PENGUIN BUSINESS

STARTUPS OF BHARAT

At twenty-seven, Aditya Arora has been recognized as a successful young entrepreneur and achiever by various national and international platforms. He has been invited to speak at 200-plus institutions globally and has won many prestigious awards for his work. Some of them include the Parliamentary Award, the Duke of Edinburgh International Award and the REX Karmaveer Chakra by the United Nations.

Some of his successful campaigns include Education Yatra, Entrepreneurship Mindset Curriculum (Government of Delhi) and Atal Innovation Mission—NITI Aayog. He is also an active content creator, known as the 'Faad guy', with over 3.5 lakh followers across social media platforms.

Currently, he is the CEO at Faad Capital (SEBI-registered CAT-1 fund of $40 million) and an angel investor in more than twenty startups. Till date, Faad has invested in over 115 startups and was recently featured in the *Economic Times*' Fastest Growing Investment Firms in India, Inc42's Top 10 Active Investors of 2024 and among the top fifteen startup investors in the country.

Surya Pasricha is the founder of BaatCheet Media, where he blends storytelling and technology to build impactful brands. He has led campaigns for names like SBI Foundation and Youth for India and has also worked with top agencies such as Rediffusion and Magnon TBWA, handling brands such as Valvoline, Daikin and WaterAid.

A passionate researcher, he won the Best Paper Award for his study on whistle-blowing intentions among Indian nurses. At twenty, he was one of the youngest Indians selected for the prestigious MIT Bootcamps.

Surya also hosts the *Discussions Delivered* podcast, featuring thirty-plus global leaders—from the principal economist of the Government of New Zealand to TEDx speakers and *Forbes* 30 Under 30 honorees—reaching listeners in fifteen countries.

With more than 7 million views on LinkedIn, his interests span advertising, observational storytelling, bingeing on world news and startup stories and public speaking. He has delivered keynotes at Delhi University, University of Mumbai and other forums.

He is also the man behind the viral Zomato cover letter that caught nationwide attention, and his work has been featured in prominent digital forums covering marketing, media and advertising.

STARTUPS OF BHARAT

Stories of India's Million-Dollar Founders Under Thirty

ADITYA ARORA
SURYA PASRICHA

PENGUIN
BUSINESS

An imprint of Penguin Random House

PENGUIN BUSINESS

Penguin Business is an imprint of the Penguin Random House group of companies whose addresses can be found at global.penguinrandomhouse.com

Published by Penguin Random House India Pvt. Ltd
4th Floor, Capital Tower 1, MG Road,
Gurugram 122 002, Haryana, India

Penguin
Random House
India

First published in Penguin Business by Penguin Random House India 2025

Illustrations by Anish Bharat Kadam and BaatCheet Media

10 9 8 7 6

ISBN 9780143467380

Typeset in Adobe Caslon Pro by MAP Systems, Bengaluru, India
Printed at Replika Press Pvt. Ltd, India

www.penguin.co.in

FSC
www.fsc.org
MIX
Paper | Supporting responsible forestry
FSC™ C016779

Contents

Foreword

Bharat is a land of opportunities. It is the hearth of young, ignited minds that are vibrant with ideas and energies. However, the path to success in India is not easy and throws down many hurdles and challenges in its pursuit. There is a predetermined and often forcibly thrust expectation of education, career and family. But in recent years, a wave of entrepreneurship has challenged this set pattern, paving the way for a fresh mantra for success. As we sit down to write this foreword, we are filled with a sense of awe and admiration for these entrepreneurs, who have paved the way for a new India. 117. Yes, India has 117 unicorn startups (companies valued at more than $1 billion). What is so special about this, you ask?

This number was just thirty-one in 2019.[1] Since then, not only have we grown eighty-six other unicorns, but these billion-dollar gems have also created 2.84 million new jobs.[2] This has contributed to 10–15 per cent of India's GDP growth. But there is an issue.

As per Goldman Sachs, India needs 10 million new jobs every year.[3] And startups have to step up their game by almost 4x to achieve that. Undoubtedly, the private sector and government would chip in too, although the pace at which startups create jobs is unmatchable. But there is a dichotomy. In a workforce of close to a billion people, India has only 15.5 lakh people working in startups. While India is the youngest startup nation, with 72 per cent of founders below age thirty-five, a large part of our youth still is not into startups.[4]

There is also some brilliant news. As per the Global University Entrepreneurial Spirits Students Survey (GUESSS) 2023–24, 14 per cent of Indian students plan to start their own business immediately after graduation, and 31.4 per cent of students want to start five years after graduation, against a global average of 30 per cent.[5] Yes, the Indian youth is ready to roar and start their ventures but need the proper guidance and knowledge.

This is the objective and purpose of this book—to demystify entrepreneurship and present practical insights through fifteen case studies of young and multimillion-dollar entrepreneurs under thirty.

Whether it is about finding the right problem to solve, deploying technology to solve that problem, setting the price to the solution of that problem or acquiring the first 100 customers, this book covers step-by-step journeys of entrepreneurs such as Alakh Pandey and Prateek Maheshwari from Physics Wallah, Shashvat Nakrani from BharatPe, Varun and Tarun Gupta from Boult, Anubhav Dubey and Anand Nayak from Chai Sutta Bar, Sunny Garg, Shaifali Jain and Archit Chauhan from Crib, Neetu Yadav, Kirti Jangra and Libin V. Babu from Animall and many others.

Here is the most fascinating part about all of them: Almost everybody started their entrepreneurial journeys from college and are now running multimillion-dollar and even billion-dollar companies. They are still very young and have already seen and created the path to success. We are not against oldies, but we wanted to cover these youngsters because they can better represent what it means to start a multimillion-dollar startup under thirty.

Still not convinced? Well, give us two more minutes.

How Is This Book Different?

It is NOT your regular business studies book. This attempt is not a motivational speech where we just share the story of entrepreneurs. It is a ringside view into what they were going through during each journey, so you learn something to implement practically, not just get inspired and confused later on.

For example—How did Alakh and Prateek build the right mindset to scale Physics Wallah to a unicorn valued at $2.8 billion? How did Shashvat of BharatPe acquire his first 100 users? How did Vedant crack distribution of the hot-selling sneakers?

We have tried our best to infuse each chapter and each phase of entrepreneurship with a simple, story-based format, providing timeless lessons that apply to various areas of life, and thereby making the book relevant to entrepreneurs and non-entrepreneurs. At the end of every chapter, is a learning framework called RISING. The RISING framework—Roadblock, Ideation, Strategy, Implementation, Nakad (Money) and Growth—would be a step-by-step guide for budding and experienced entrepreneurs. We have also included an exercise at the end of each chapter for readers to solve before reading the next chapter. Yes, we call this a SIMULATION and not a book.

Now, we have made our case. So, how should you read this?

Read this book like a series you are watching where no two episodes are related, as every story is about a fresh character and situation. So, you can pick up any chapter and binge-read it. Whenever you feel stuck, flip to the chapter that fits your current challenge while building your startup or doubt that you have—IDEA, PROBLEM, PRICE, REVENUE and even MINDSET. We have it all covered. This book is here to guide you, no matter where you are in your entrepreneurial path.

Anyone interested in startups or even only thinking about taking the plunge will find something for themselves in this book.

Now, all surprises should never be revealed at once.

Should they?

So, players, get ready for Level 1 of the Simulation.

1

It All Begins with a Problem

The Story of Animall from 0 to Rs 4000 Crore in Transaction Value

Animall[1] is a peer-to-peer platform for cattle trading. In two years, they have reached eight million dairy farmers and crossed Rs 4000 crore in transaction value. The mission is to connect cattle buyers and sellers across India and enable dairy farmers to establish a source of income. Animall wants to usher in the next White Revolution that will impact over a billion lives. They have raised more than Rs 150 crore from Peak XV (erstwhile Sequoia Capital India & SEA), Nexus Venture Partners, SIG Venture Capital, Omnivore, Beenext, Rocketship.vc, WEH Ventures and other prominent investors.

Imagine standing on a battlefield, facing opponents armed with different weapons. You have just a sword. Who would you attack first?

While this situation might sound like a medieval fantasy, it resembles the process of generating ideas that, like opponents, come at you fast and diverse. Each one shines with its unique potential, making it challenging to choose which to pursue. But fear not, aspiring entrepreneur, for just like brave warriors, you too can conquer this realm of possibilities.

Welcome to the world of startups.

This chapter will start your entrepreneurial journey by helping you understand the phrase 'ideating and finding the right problem to solve'. After all, startups are all about solving problems.

Uber is doing it for transportation, Zomato is solving hunger and Paytm is doing it for financial security and efficiency. If you can ideate and solve the right problem, you have a chance to become successful.

But what are some of the salient features of the problem that help in the success of a startup?

- The problem has to address a big market.
- The problem has to be repetitive so that a startup can earn regular income by solving it.
- The problem should be a 'must' and not 'good'. People pay for necessities but have a choice in comfort.

In this chapter, we'll delve into the story of three real-life entrepreneurs, who faced the same constellation of choices as you. They also set out to solve a problem that was big, repetitive, and a 'must' to solve. So, get ready to learn from their practical insights and turn your ideas into reality.

Massive Rural Community

According to the World Bank, as of 2023, approximately 63.64 per cent of India's total population lives in rural areas,[2] with a significant portion relying on agriculture for their livelihoods. However, agricultural income is often subject to uncertainty due to various factors, such as unpredictable weather patterns, market fluctuations and supply chain challenges.

On the other hand, dairy farming is a treasure trove that promises steady revenues. With over 307.6 million cattle in India as per a survey published on Statista.com in 2024,[3] this is an industry with plenty of room available for innovation.

Unveiling the Problem

So, why hasn't everyone jumped into this seemingly large market?

The answer is—It's no easy feat.

Cattle trading, a vital part of dairy farming, happens in distant 'Cattle Fairs'. Farmers pay entry fees and face the risk of no sales. These 'fairs' happen at places far away from villages, and the farmer has no certainty of a buyer-seller match. Imagine the struggle! Still, a few entrepreneurs want to solve for and build for this seemingly 'unglamorous' industry.

Within these challenges lies an opportunity.

The 'unglamorous' work often leads to the most impactful solutions.

The Journey of Animall: Shunning Herd Mentality to Sell Cattle

Meet Kirti Jangra, Neetu Yadav and Libin V. Babu, three young entrepreneurs, who embarked on a magical journey with Animall. Their mission? To transform the lives of dairy farmers across India by revolutionizing cattle trading.

Planting the Seeds of Ideation

It all began with an internal hackathon at Pratilipi, an online storytelling platform, where Neetu, working as a product manager, sensed the sparks of innovation in the air. The theme was: 'Building for the Next One Billion Users'.

Now imagine a real-life hackathon or any other competition for that matter.

There are lots of tables. At each table, there's a group of people working on their next big idea. Some are good at writing computer code, some are good at designing how things will look and others are good at turning ideas into real products.

The room is buzzing with excitement. People are typing on their laptops, talking to each other and coming up with new ideas. It's a diverse group, with multifarious skills and backgrounds, all working together to create something special.

The theme, 'Building for the Next One Billion Users', is like a challenge. It's asking everyone to think big and come up with solutions that can help a lot of people, who haven't had access to technology before.

Time seems to fly by as people work on their projects. They're so focused that they forget about sleep. They drink lots of coffee to stay awake and keep working. The room is always busy, with teams refining their ideas, making them better, and getting ready to show them to others.

Neetu was busy hustling, too. As she pondered over the idea of creating a solution for the next one billion users, one thought kept recurring in her mind—the farmer.

According to her, the next one billion users coming online would largely consist of people from rural areas, and farmers would be at the forefront and cusp of this revolution.

Now, having grown up in a farming household in Shahpura, Jaipur, Neetu knew firsthand the significance of dairy farming in a farmer's life. She understood that a substantial portion of an agrarian household's income came from dairy farming, making it a consistent and predictable revenue source. Yet, she realized that the dairy industry remained largely untapped, unlike the agriculture sector, which already had numerous companies working on various solutions.

Curiosity drove Neetu to delve deeper into the dairy industry. She started reading extensively, trying to understand the nuances and dynamics of this massive, yet overlooked, market.

Although she had a bird's eye view on ideas that could potentially go on to becoming big, she was facing difficulties in identifying the right problem.

Roaming in the Idea Garden

The path to a brilliant idea isn't linear. Neetu researched extensively to understand the dynamics of the dairy industry. She realized that farmers relied heavily on cattle trading for stable income. However, there were fewer dairy farmers per cattle. Even Brazil had two million dairy farmers for 100 million cattle. This insight became the cornerstone of Animall's trajectory.

Neetu continued her journey with the hackathon's gruelling rounds. She started refining her idea, developing a business plan and creating a compelling pitch. Like the other participants, she faced sleepless nights and numerous revisions. The competition was fierce, and the judges' scrutiny was relentless. The pressure was on.

However, when the hackathon finally came to an end, Animall emerged as the winner, receiving both the jury and audience awards. As Neetu's vision took shape, she teamed up with her best friend, Kirti, and they began their adventure.

Drilling Deep into the Problem

In August 2019, Neetu, Kirti and Libin started talking to multiple farmers together to validate their perspectives on the problem. They identified that the problem ran even larger. After talking to so many farmers, the trio knew that they had to rely on multiple micro-insights while building for a macro-vision that was going to impact billions of lives out there.

At this time, they noticed and realized that the income from dairy farming is super consistent, unlike the uncertainty faced by farmers in the agriculture sector, where rain or extreme weather could easily damage crops, leading to financial losses. The dairy farmers' reliance on cattle as an asset started becoming even more apparent to the trio as these farmers encountered situations like marriages or other significant events in their family life that required a substantial amount of money.

During such times, cattle could be sold, providing a quick and reliable source of funds.

However, the existing system of selling cattle at traditional cattle fairs posed significant challenges for farmers. As mentioned earlier, these were:

- Cattle fairs were often situated far from the farmers' villages, making transportation of cattle both cumbersome and expensive.
- There was a mandatory entry fee for these cattle fairs that led the farmers into a sunk cost fallacy.

After getting the validation on the problem, the three co-founders mustered the courage to leave their jobs in 2019 and thus, the Animall app was born.

Overcoming Scepticism and Challenges of the Problem

At first, selling and buying cattle through an app seemed impossible. But Neetu's, Kirti's and Libin's passion for solving problems through technology drove them forward. Leveraging their engineering background, they built a user-friendly interface and created a virtual marketplace that connected farmers and buyers. Farmers could easily upload information about their cattle. On the other hand, potential buyers could browse these listings, assess the cattle's details and connect directly with sellers through the app.

Everything that they did was based on first principles.

Now, what are 'first principles', you ask?

Well, first principles are like the basic ingredients in a recipe.

Just as you need to understand the key elements in baking a cake (flour, eggs, sugar), first principles are fundamental concepts that help you solve problems and innovate.

They're the building blocks that allow you to break down complex problems, understand how things work and come up with creative solutions.

So, whether you are baking a cake or working on an entrepreneurial project, remember to start with the basics—the macro insights, the first principles—and build from there.

The 'Problem' Getting Answered

Through careful understanding, the trio eliminated cattle fairs. Animall significantly reduced entry barriers for farmers, making cattle transactions more efficient and cost-effective. This newfound accessibility allowed farmers to explore a larger market and find better deals for their cattle.

As more farmers joined the platform, the cattle listings became more diverse. Animall's reach expanded beyond the borders of individual villages, connecting farmers from different states and regions by leveraging smart techniques such as YouTube marketing. This not only increased the chances of finding suitable buyers but also fostered a sense of community among dairy farmers across the country.

The impact of the venture's cattle transaction services was so transformative that the farmers started experiencing newfound financial freedom, knowing that their cattle could be easily converted into 'cash cows' during times of need. The platform's efficiency eliminated barriers and connected farmers from different regions. The convenience and efficiency of the platform has also encouraged more farmers to invest in cattle farming as it provides a reliable means of income.

* * *

With this problem getting solved, does that mean it is over?

Not really—this is just the start of Animall as they prepare to solve other problems plaguing the cattle industry.

Neetu, Kirti and Libin's strategic approach of attacking one pillar at a time has yielded significant results. By focusing on the specific pain point of cattle transactions, they have managed to create a profound positive impact on the lives of farmers. But they are not ready to rest on their laurels just yet.

With each milestone, they have gained more insights into the dairy industry and have identified new challenges to address. Their success in cattle transactions has given them the confidence to explore other problems in the dairy ecosystem. In fact, as mentioned earlier, they have already started working on solving other problems affecting the dairy industry. One such problem they are actively looking to solve is offering hassle-free and affordable cattle insurance.

The impact these founders have already created is just a glimpse of what is yet to come.

As they say, 'The day an entrepreneur stops solving problems is the day they stop being called an "entrepreneur".'

In just a short span of two years, Animall has reached more than eight million dairy farmers with a Rs 7500 crore of gross transactional value (GTV). Their dairy farmers have rated them 4.8 out of 5, and 65+ per cent of these dairy farmers refer Animall to at least one friend monthly.[4]

Through this story, we saw how a business idea emerges from a problem and how an entrepreneur goes deep into truly understanding the problem. Entrepreneurs need a ground view of how they would solve the customer's pain points.

Enough gyaan, let us look at our takeaways from this chapter that will help you in your journey.

Key Takeaways

- **Identify Micro-Insights**: Dig deep to find the hidden pain points in a market or industry. These insights can pave the way to understanding the root cause of problems around you.
- **Focus on Specific Pain Points**: Don't try to solve every problem. Tackle one challenge at a time, just like Animall did with cattle transactions.
- **Know Your Ideal Customer**: Understand your target audience intimately. This knowledge will help you understand the specific pain points to solve.
- **Stay Open to Change**: Be prepared to evolve and adapt. The problem changes with time. For example, online food delivery is not a problem today. Use technology to innovate constantly. The journey won't be linear, but each step is progress.

So, What Should You Do Next?

Well, write down ten problems around you, rank them in order of their difficulty (how big you think they are) and then write down the micro-insights and specific pain points for the top two.

Given below is a framework called RISING, which will guide you through Animall's journey in a nutshell:

Roadblock	**Ideal Customer**	**Solution**	**Innovation**	**Nakad (Money)**	**Growth**
Inefficient cattle trading system	Dairy farmers and cattle owners	Online marketplace for cattle buyers and sellers	User-friendly interface accessible to farmers with limited technological know-how Dynamic listing, vernacular targeting	Rs 25 charged from the farmers per veterinary consultation Monetizing through the prime seller feature (Rs 350 per cattle or Rs 100 for 3 cattle)	Expanding platform to connect farmers from different regions, leveraging smart techniques such as YouTube marketing, creating a diverse range of cattle listings Fostering a sense of community among dairy farmers and increasing their financial freedom

2

The Million-Dollar Idea

How Did bluelearn Scale to 1,50,000 Members?

One of India's largest student communities, bluelearn provides a one-stop platform for students to learn new skills, network with peers and grow as an individual. With over 1,50,000 community members, 5500 schools and colleges and 650-plus recruiters, they are on a mission to empower the next generation to discover better ways to learn, earn and network. They have also raised USD 3.5 million in a seed funding round led by Elevation Capital and Lightspeed Venture Partners.[1]

Building on the previous chapter's exploration of ideation and finding the right problem to solve, this chapter will deepen your journey into the entrepreneurial landscape. After reading the title of this chapter, you might have a question in mind: What is the difference between a problem and an idea? Well, an idea is a general concept, while the 'right problem' is a specific, well-defined challenge that addresses a significant need and has the potential for a viable solution.

While startups are ultimately about problem-solving, the success of an entrepreneur's venture depends on choosing the right idea to pursue.

But what defines an idea as the 'right' one for your startup? Let's dissect the characteristics:

- **Market Appeal:** Your chosen idea should resonate with a substantial market, like selecting a book that appeals to a broad readership. The wider the idea's appeal, the greater the potential for success.

For example, consider how the rise of digital payments in India—driven by initiatives like UPI and the increasing adoption of smartphones—created a vast market for mobile payment apps. Apps like BharatPe, the story of which we have covered in a later chapter of this book, have gained widespread acceptance, offering merchants a convenient and secure way to conduct financial transactions.

- **Sustainable Demand:** Just as a timeless classic remains in demand year after year, your startup idea should cater to an ongoing need. This sustained demand ensures that your venture can thrive and grow.

India's growing population and increasing awareness of healthcare needs have created a sustained demand for healthcare services. Startups like Practo and 1mg have capitalized on this demand by providing online consultation, medicine delivery and health-related information to users across the country.

- **Necessity, Not Just Luxury:** Your selected idea should ideally be a 'must-have' for your target audience, not just a 'nice-to-have'. People readily invest in necessities but exercise discretion when it comes to luxuries. Your solution should address a fundamental need, like a book that leaves an indelible mark.

Access to affordable housing is a pressing need for a significant portion of India's population. Startups like MagicBricks are addressing this necessity by providing affordable housing solutions and streamlining the rental process.

As we progress through this chapter, we'll embark on a journey of exploration, drawing from real-life experiences of an EdTech entrepreneur. His story will illuminate the path to identifying the idea that aligns with the three critical attributes mentioned above, equipping you with the knowledge and insight needed to breathe life into your own startup concept.

So, prepare to deepen your understanding of the entrepreneurial landscape, for the treasure trove of startup ideas beckons, and your success hinges on your ability to select the idea that resonates most profoundly with both your target market and your entrepreneurial spirit.

Massive Student Population but Hardly Any in Top Colleges!

Now, if you come from an ordinary college in India, chances are that you might have faced or would face the problem of lack of access to the right mentorship, resources and more. Since entrance exams to elite institutions and universities in India are super hard to crack, both due to the difficulty level as well as the number of aspirants applying to these colleges, not many students are left with good options.

For example, if we consider IITs, more than a million students apply to get into these institutions of prestige, but there are only a few thousand seats. The case is similar with most of the other prestigious colleges that require students to go through a competitive exam; in most cases, this stage decides their fate.

The disparity in the total number of students applying and the number of seats is quite huge, which leads to students either taking a drop year or joining other tier-2 or tier-3 colleges, where the education may not be as good as at elite institutions like the IITs, IIMs or AIIMS.

Selecting the Right Startup Idea

Choosing the right startup idea is super important, especially in a country like ours. The business scene in our country is always changing, with new technologies, trends and customer preferences popping up all the time.

So, one's startup idea needs to be spot-on as it sets the stage for everything.

One should think about how the market keeps shifting. What's hot today might not be tomorrow.

If you pick the right idea, it'll be like having a flexible plan that can adjust to changes. But if your idea isn't good, you could be stuck in a tough spot or even have to start from scratch.

The ability to pivot, adapt and innovate is essential for startups, and the initial idea plays a pivotal role in determining the feasibility and adaptability of the business model.

Your startup idea also tells people what your business is all about. It's like the unique personality of your business. It helps you stand out in a crowd. Plus, it decides how you'll reach your customers—whether you'll sell to other businesses or directly to people, whether you'll focus on something that's never been done before or try to do something better or cheaper.

And remember, the product or service that comes from your idea is only as good as the idea itself.

So, by making sure you've got the right startup idea, you're also making sure that you're on the right track from the very beginning.

Now, let's dive deeper into how the startup entrepreneur featured in this chapter navigated the journey of selecting the right startup idea.

While there are many startups operating within the upskilling EdTech space in India, only a select few have been able to recognize and harness the immense potential and power of community-driven learning.

In a landscape often characterized by conventional, one-size-fits-all educational models, these innovative ventures have tussled to stand out by fostering a collaborative and inclusive environment, where learners can flourish and support one another on their educational journeys. This community-centric approach not only enriches the learning experience but also fosters a sense of belonging and empowerment, making these startups battle to become the pioneers in the realm of education and technology.

These startups have realized that learning is not a linear path but is a personal and often non-linear journey. Therefore, they tailor their offerings to cater to the unique needs and interests of each learner. This flexibility allows individuals to explore subjects that genuinely resonate with them and in this way, pursue their passions.

The Journey of bluelearn: Empowering Every Individual to Make an Impact

On their first day at BITS Pilani, Goa, as the massive entry gates to the beautiful campus near sprawling beaches opened, Harish, Shreyans and the entire BITSIAN family thrummed with excitement. After all, they had been on a long and incredibly tough journey of studying hard in Class 11 and Class 12 to live this dream that they now be held in person.

Just as any regular college kid would explore the campus, Harish and Shreyans embarked on the same tour. They walked around the premises, checked on their classes, went to the hostel and also tried out the hostel mess—the place where they would be filling their stomachs for the next four years.

Many enthusiastic and passionate students were dawdling around, some contemplating why they didn't get into an IIT, some thinking where all they would roam around in Goa, some finding ideal spots on campus to hang out with their friends and some trying to network with professors, researchers, students or anyone they could catch hold of.

The students slowly started settling in, and it was finally time for the first day of classes on the campus sprawled over more than 80 lakh square feet.

As part of the induction, professors asked for every student's introduction. The process, however, had to be done in alphabetical order. So, students whose names began with 'A' introduced themselves first, followed by the 'Bs', then the 'Cs' and so on. By the time Harish's turn came, he had already made up his mind as to what he would say. Finally, it was his turn, and he blurted out: 'Hi guys, so I am Harish and my hobby is to build companies.'

There was a moment of silence in the room, and he realized that everyone was flabbergasted by his words. They probably could not believe that when most students his age are having fun, going out for parties, chilling with friends and thinking about securing a job—especially in a 'MAANG' (acronym for Meta, Amazon, Apple, Netflix or Google) company—this guy had just said that his hobby was to build companies. Like, really?

Wasn't it a bit unusual to hear from a young guy? Something truly extraordinary?

The trance was broken by a pat on his back. He turned around to see Shreyans, who would, in future, be his friend and co-founder in many ventures to come.

After that day, their bond only grew stronger and they went to events, parties and everywhere else together. Being two dynamic and restless students in college, they wanted to build something meaningful and, at the same time, figure out ways to make money out of it, so that maybe they could pay their own college fees.

Funding one's own college degree seems quite hard but remember—'When the going gets tough, the tough get going.'

While Harish started upping his graphic design skills, Shreyans, on the other hand, began an internship with a media agency. Both performed exceedingly well and acquired core competencies in a wide array of skills, from creating websites through WordPress to learning a bit about coding and more.

They lapped up whatever training came their way to satiate their hunger to learn. Both were very restless and driven, and it seemed like there was almost nothing on this planet that could stop them.

> You see, all successful entrepreneurs have this one common trait—They all are hungry, and their hunger never gets satiated, even when they had the tastiest meal out there.
>
> In fact, the one factor that differentiates a great company from an ordinary one is the founder. The common thread running through all successful startups is, therefore, the founder.
>
> Successful founders like the entire buffet, not any one dish in particular—and owing to this everlasting and endless hunger for learning, they have to grow their basket of skills proportionately.

On this upskilling journey, Harish eventually started freelancing and taking up a lot of graphic design gigs, However, he soon realized that he didn't want to see himself as a graphic designer in the future. So, he switched paths and started his own YouTube channel by the name of 'Curious Harish', where he initially started posting about topics like 'How to earn money through freelancing'. He realized that there lay a golden opportunity in the YouTube space that he could greatly exploit to his benefit, taking advantage of what BITS Pilani had to offer. He noticed that not enough relevant videos about BITS Pilani were available on YouTube. However, there were a lot of search queries for BITS Pilani. The realization of this huge gap led him to start creating videos on this theme.[2] He decided to capture his entire campus on camera, covering every possible event that took place on the grounds.

To his surprise, he found no success. This is when he decided to vlog about his life at BITS Pilani, Goa, showcasing every aspect of it. His videos included both the good and not-so-good things about his life at the institute. He started getting popular on YouTube as aspiring students were curious to know about BITS Pilani and the student life there. 'Curious Harish' and BITS Pilani, Goa, both blew up. The numbers were massive, and so was the traction.

But this was just the beginning and there was a long road ahead.

How Did Harish Become an Entrepreneur?

One day, Harish called up Shreyans and asked him, 'Would you like to work on a website project?' Shreyans, having written blogs and learnt WordPress development, agreed to take it on.

They officially started making chatbots for companies that needed them, especially for clients based in the US. The duo named this venture 'Huloq Chatbots'. The word 'Huloq' had struck Harish while he was working out various permutations and combinations to name the newly formed company. He had an instant liking to this word combination—and to their delight, the domain name was available.

Initially, Harish and Shreyans did a brief competitive analysis of the industry and made the product for anyone and everyone. Later, they realized that they needed to specialize in a particular domain if they wanted the company to scale and grow. They dabbled with a lot of clients, tried different kinds of chatbots, iterated on various product versions and experimented with a lot of plugins and tech.

Slowly, they figured out that the pharmaceutical industry was the right sector to cater to with their chatbots. Although they went on with the venture for quite some time, they gradually comprehended certain shortcomings that obstructed the growth of the venture. The major issues faced were slowed revenue growth, as well as problems in scalability. This gradually led to the closing down of this venture.

You see, as an entrepreneur, you may have multiple ideas for multiple industries, but what matters at the end of the day is how well you execute those ideas to bring them to fruition.

Having a bunch of great ideas is just the beginning—the real magic happens when you take action and bring those ideas to life.

Execution is that process of taking your concepts and translating them into products or services that address real market needs. In a diverse and dynamic country like India, where opportunities are plenty but so are challenges, effective execution is the key to navigating the business landscape successfully.

So, while brainstorming and ideation are crucial aspects of entrepreneurship, they must be followed by decisive action.

Turning Things Around: How They Struck Upon the Idea of bluelearn

People with an entrepreneurial mindset don't quit; they are relentless in their pursuit of making their venture work. This unwavering determination is the heartbeat of entrepreneurship. It's what separates those who dream from those who turn those dreams into reality.

Harish and Shreyans possessed the same mindset. They didn't have a great outcome with their previous venture, but as they say, 'An entrepreneur will always remain an entrepreneur.' Another famous quote by Steve Jobs goes: Stay hungry, stay foolish.[3] This aptly sums up an entrepreneur's motto.

The duo started brainstorming once again on the different problems they could possibly solve. Somehow, the problem of outdated education standards in lower-tier colleges fascinated them.

Harish and Shreyans were passionate about solving this problem of access to quality education at the college level. So, after a lot of brainstorming sessions, spending long nights in their hostel rooms and talking to people, they decided to start 'Clinify'.

The proposition was simple: To help the youth of India get the right opportunities and hands-on experiences whilst being a part of a student community, where each member is equally passionate for learning and acquiring new skills.

While the problem seemed simple to solve, it had a huge level of complexity when one decided to delve deeper.

One problem was identifying the right mentors, another was how to get students at a mass level to join their Telegram community; yet another was how to manage these students once they did join the community.

However, the budding entrepreneur duo knew that they had to start somewhere. As the great polymath Albert Schweitzer said: 'Eventually all things fall into place. Until then, laugh at the confusion, live for the moments, and know everything happens for a reason.'[4]

Harish and Shreyans took his words and started applying all they had at that time and moment to the task at hand.

However, along this journey, one more problem struck them—that their company's name was sounding 'too medical', which could cause brand identity problems later. So, they decided to tackle this right away.

They sat together periodically and just came up with a bunch of names. They went through dog names, Greek names, AI-generated names and what not—but they just could not come up with the right name for their venture.

Then suddenly they thought, 'Why not explore colours?' It started with yellow and went through an entire spectrum, but the colour blue stood out the most. If one was to look at it philosophically, this hue signifies vastness.

And so, bluelearn came to mean 'vast learning'.

What's in a Startup's Name?

In essence, a name reflects the founder's vision, is a symbol of their commitment and is a key element in shaping a venture's identity.

Although, the previous name of bluelearn—Clinify—was not a bad one, it didn't quite resound with the vision they were trying to build.

A startup's name is similar to an advertising jingle, in the sense that it plays a crucial role in creating brand recall in consumers' minds. Just as a catchy jingle can make a product or company memorable and easily recognizable, a well-chosen startup name can have the same effect.

Remember the jingle: 'Vicco turmeric nahi cosmetic, Vicco turmeric Ayurvedic cream'? Not only did it have catchy tune, but also a clear message that emphasized the natural and Ayurvedic qualities of the product. This made it not just memorable, but simultaneously communicated a unique selling proposition to consumers.

Thus, your venture's name should define your essence, encapsulate your values and resonate with your target audience, just like the 'Vicco turmeric' jingle did for its product.

The name of a startup is not just a label, but a compass that guides its journey and a language that speaks of its purpose.

Choose it wisely, for it carries the weight of your vision and the promise of your venture's legacy.

Expanding on the Idea and Turning It into a Big Company

Harish and Shreyans leveraged the power of social media, their network of friends and the alumni of BITS Pilani, Goa, to eventually spread the word and build their community. Once they cracked the initial market and got a few of their friends from other colleges to join their community, the same people appreciated the efforts of bringing them joy through regular sessions with industry experts and influencers, and the chill sessions in which they aimed to create an open and a safe space for students to discuss their problems. Now, word about the 'community' started spreading like wildfire.

Their user base expanded with time and also awareness amongst their target audience. Having built a substantial audience base so far, they were eager to grow further to help drive the change in the Indian educational paradigm. So, the duo started looking for investment opportunities and approached multiple investors, ranging from angels to VCs to pre-seed funds.

Today, bluelearn has gone on to become the largest community of tomorrow's builders, with 1,50,000-plus members from over 5500 colleges and startups across more than twenty countries, while also organically growing at a 30 per cent rate month-to-month. It has also raised USD 3.5 million in a seed funding round led by Elevation Capital and Lightspeed Venture Partners.

The future of education is surely in the right hands.

As entrepreneurs, Harish and Shreyans demonstrated resilience and determination by not giving up, even in the face of multiple failures. When their first few ideas around providing graphic designing services, making chatbots for organizations and the name 'Clinify' didn't work out, they didn't lose their motivation.

Instead, they decided to change the name to bluelearn, signifying 'vast learning', and maintained their enthusiasm and motivation, continuously experimenting with use cases (different user needs and potential challenges) in the face of the ever-evolving market dynamics.

This approach highlights a key aspect of entrepreneurship—**the willingness to learn from failures and iterate on ideas until success is achieved.**

A lot of times, when your ideas start falling flat one after another, it can be an incredibly frustrating and demoralizing experience as an entrepreneur. The entrepreneurial journey is often characterized by its highs and lows, and it is during these challenging moments that your resilience and adaptability are put to the test. Rather than viewing these setbacks as failures, see them as opportunities for refinement and growth. Reevaluate your business strategies, listen to customer feedback and be open to making the necessary adjustments.

Last but not least, don't back down.

By keeping their *josh* (enthusiasm) high and remaining persistent, Harish and Shreyans ultimately found a path that led to success in finding the right startup idea—bluelearn.

Their story is testament to the fact that setbacks are a natural part of entrepreneurship, but they can also be 'vast learning' experiences on the road to success.

Key Takeaways

- **Market Validation:** Thoroughly validate your startup idea in the market by conducting market research, seeking feedback from potential customers and assessing its fit within the current industry landscape.
- **Problem-Solution Fit:** Ensure a strong alignment between your chosen idea and the real pain points or needs of your target audience. The more precisely your idea addresses these pain points, the greater its potential for success. Remember, every solution is not the ideal solution.
- **Scalability Potential:** Assess the scalability of your startup idea. Evaluate whether it has the potential to grow and capture a significant share of the market over time, ensuring long-term viability and success. In the race to win in the short-term, don't forget that you are there for a marathon.
- **Foster an Entrepreneurial Mindset**: Your determination and adaptability as a founder would be critical to a startup's success. Founders who remain hungry for knowledge and are willing to pivot can navigate challenges effectively.

So, What Should You Do Next?

Write down ten startup ideas that could help you solve the problems you identified in the previous chapter and rank them in accordance with how big you think they are. Select the best two and write down your reasons for selecting those.

Also, like in the previous chapter, given below is the framework called RISING, which will guide you through bluelearn's journey in a nutshell:

Roadblock	**Ideal Customer**	**Solution**	**Innovation**	**Nakad (Money)**	**Growth**
Challenges in maintaining and managing a community Challenges in expanding the user base	Students studying in colleges and universities	bluelearn, a student community that provides a one-stop platform for students to learn new skills, network with peers and grow as an individual	Addressing specific needs, such as hiring from and mentorship to student communities	Focused paid communities Charging the companies that hire from bluelearn	Expansion in international markets Full stack solution for any student community

3

Prototype from Scratch

Inside View of Pepper Content to Scale to 1,20,000-Plus Creators

Pepper Content[1] is an AI-based content mediation platform that connects talented writers to organizations that require content. It was founded in 2017 by Anirudh Singla and Rishabh Shekhar in their dorm room at BITS Pilani. Today, their platform boasts of more than a million content projects delivered, 1,20,000-plus creators and $3.5 million in creator earnings. It has evolved from a content marketplace to an AI-based enterprise solution, serving clients such as McKinsey & Company, Unilever, P&G, Adani Group and more.

We live in an era when the internet dominates our daily lives, and let's be honest, almost everyone watches something or the other on YouTube. Whether it's bingeing podcasts, funny videos or tutorials, YouTube has become a central part of how we consume content. But did you know that this platform, which currently ranks as the second-most popular search engine in the world, didn't start this way?

Back in 2005, YouTube was conceived as a dating site. Yep, the original idea was to help people upload videos of themselves and find their perfect match. In fact, hardly anyone used it for dating. But instead of calling it quits, the founders noticed something remarkable—users were uploading random videos.

This insight led them to pivot and refine their idea. In May 2005, when the beta site first went up, it started receiving about 30,000 visits every day.[2] On 15 December 2005, YouTube made its formal debut, offering more than two million video views daily. In October 2006, Google revealed that it had paid an estimated $1.65 billion for YouTube.[3]

This story is an example of prototyping done right—starting with an idea, testing it, learning from user behaviour and making the necessary changes to create something people genuinely want.

As we were discussing the content that would adorn the pages of this book and particularly of this chapter, we had two objectives in mind, one of which we would be sharing in the pages ahead. One of the objectives was to help you explore and learn how to build your prototype, gather feedback and iterate until you have something extraordinary.

Because who knows? Maybe your startup idea could be the next big thing.

Let's Start by Understanding What Exactly Is a Prototype?

It's essentially a preliminary version or model of a product or service created to test and validate key aspects of your startup idea. A prototype is often mistaken for a similar term—MVP or Minimum Viable Product. While a prototype is a test and validator of key elements and functionalities of your idea, an MVP is designed to be deployed to real users to gather feedback and validate assumptions about your business model, customer needs and market demand. In simpler terms, a prototype is like a rough sketch of your idea, while an MVP is a more polished version that you can show to potential users or investors.

A prototype is crucial to a startup's success, as it is the foundation upon which the next steps of the startup depend.

Let's take a closer look at Uber's beginnings to understand how prototyping helps achieve success by validating the idea. Uber, founded in 2009 by Travis Kalanick and Garrett Camp, revolutionized the transportation industry by introducing a new model for on-demand ride sharing. Camp originally came up with the idea for Uber while attending a tech conference in Paris. Frustrated with the difficulty of finding a taxi, he envisioned a service where users could request a ride with a button on their smartphones. However, Uber started with something other than the sophisticated app we know today. Its early stages involved a process of experimentation and prototyping to validate whether the idea would even work or not. In Uber's case, the prototype was not a high-tech app but a simple SMS-based service.

Camp and Kalanick built a basic system that allowed users to request a black car service by sending a text message. This prototype, known as UberCab at the time, served as a 'proof of concept', demonstrating the feasibility and potential of the idea while validating the demand for on-demand transportation.

Uber's founders later graduated from this prototype to building an MVP to gather feedback from early users and iterate on the concept before investing in a more robust platform. As they refined their idea, they gradually developed the Uber App we all know of and use today.

Now that we have explored what a prototype is and one primary reason why it matters for startups, let's dive into some other key reasons for its importance.

Prototyping helps in:

1. **Refining Ideas**: When you get to see your idea come to life in a tangible form, it helps in visualizing the concept and refining on it if needed.
2. **Validating Assumptions**: It helps you kill the flaws before they kill you (your idea and business).
3. **Saving Time and Money**: Before going all in to create a full-fledged product, a prototype helps experiment with different features, designs and functionalities without committing extensive resources
4. **Attracting Investors and Partners by giving them an early look and feel of the product:** A prototype can also be beneficial when an entrepreneur needs to make massive improvement to the UI/UX.

Remember? In the beginning of the chapter, we said that we had two objectives for writing this chapter, one of which we already revealed earlier. If you are guessing what the second objective is, well you don't have to wait any further.

As we were doing our research for this chapter, we noticed one critical gap: hardly any literature on prototyping was written from the lens of an entrepreneur in India. Yes! Most of the blogs, research papers, etc. covered Western examples.

Given that this book is all about the essence of Bharat and its entrepreneurs, we had to interview someone who had not just created massive value with their startup but also started with one vision and then moved to an iterative model of their initial product.

So, let us now dive deep into the journey of Anirudh Singla, the founder and CEO of Pepper Content, which initially started as a content marketplace but later pivoted to an enterprise-level model.

This fascinating story of prototyping and how Anirudh went on scaling Pepper Content from a dorm room in BITS Pilani to 2500-plus customers and a creator network of more than 1,20,000 creators will definitely enthrall you.

From Dorm Rooms to Board Rooms

It was a bright, sunny day and also results day for the BITS Pilani entrance exam. A boy named Anirudh Singla was eagerly waiting for his results in his room. Soon, they were announced—excited to see them, Anirudh opened his laptop and logged onto the website. There it was—Anirudh had gotten into the prestigious BITS Pilani for a degree in electronics and electrical engineering. As soon as he entered college, Anirudh was driven by his goal to finance his own education. To earn roughly Rs 2.5 lakh in two months, he turned to freelancing on platforms like Fiverr and Upwork, primarily catering to the US market.

Juggling freelance work with an internship at YourStory, Anirudh dedicated almost nineteen hours daily to meet this financial target.

During this time, Anirudh realized there was no talent marketplace in the country, despite a vast population of creative individuals. Returning to college, he teamed up with a few friends to build a content marketplace platform called Pepper. Through his freelancing experience, Anirudh had learned two crucial lessons—the importance of talent and the significant demand for a talent marketplace in India. Initially, Pepper Content was envisaged as a content marketplace that would connect businesses with freelance writers, designers and creators to fulfill their content needs.

Now, Anirudh was quite active in his college's clubs and committees as he was always driven by his dreams of finding the next big opportunity and funding his own college education. Anirudh is quoted in an article by Global Indian, 'With his entrepreneurial vision, he found a small digital marketing agency that needed 250 articles of 500 words each on car parts. "We quoted 75 paise per word, which is around **Rs 375 per article**. However, the customer insisted on 10 paise per word—you can't outsource it at that rate, no writer will agree. But we wanted a statistical advantage, and we were just starting out, so we negotiated it to 15 paise per word."'[4]

However, as the demand for content surged during the pandemic, particularly among larger enterprises, Pepper Content recognized the limitations of this original model. The traditional freelance marketplace approach often led to inefficiencies, such as lengthy negotiations and the challenge of managing multiple freelancers across various projects. Companies were scaling their content needs rapidly, and a more streamlined solution was necessary.

Now, as much as pivots are important in startups, they are important in life as well. Even we pivoted several times in this chapter going from one draft to another. But let us focus on Pepper for now! Let us look behind the screens at how they took a big step and still ended up raising over 100 crore from investors.

How Did Pepper Content Shift Gears with a New Prototype?

Creating a prototype is a pretty long process at Pepper Content, as it should be. Anirudh spends about seven to eight days each month meeting with customers. For example, when we interviewed him, he already had fifteen or twenty customer meetings scheduled in Bengaluru over five days. These meetings are crucial for them as they help understand the ecosystem, share their updates and, most importantly, listen to customer problems. This feedback shapes Pepper's product roadmap, positioning and market strategy. Ultimately, the customer defines what kind of company they will become.

Once these problems are heard, the team needs to go back to the drawing board and understand which feedback to work on and which not to.

Sometimes, entrepreneurs get too much feedback on their initial prototypes and picking and choosing which ones to act on is tough. When we posed this question to Anirudh, he said, 'Deciding which feedback to act on is often a gut feeling, influenced by understanding what truly matters. It's crucial to have a team that can provide objective perspectives. For any development, unless there is significant customer demand backed by a willingness to pay, we don't proceed. This approach ensures our efforts are aligned with real market needs.'

The prototyping journey begins with creating the wireframes and UI and then showing these to twenty-odd customers to get specific feedback on usability. Now what do the terms 'wireframe' and 'UI' mean, you ask? The wireframe is a simple outline of a digital product's layout. It shows where elements like buttons and menus will go, focusing on structure rather than design. On the other hand, the UI or the User Interface is the actual design of the product. It includes all the visual elements including the colours, fonts and images that users see and interact with. This process of constructing the wireframe and the UI helped Pepper Content avoid the pitfall of initial customer fascination that doesn't translate into long-term use. Their streamlined process ensured they developed features that meet real customer needs and are mindful of the Pepper team's time and resources.

Also, to achieve this complete shift in focus from a marketplace to an enterprise focused model, Pepper Content introduced several key innovations.

1. It leveraged generative AI technology, which allowed businesses to create high-quality content quickly and efficiently. This AI-driven approach not only sped up the content creation process but

also ensured that the content aligned with the brand's voice and messaging.

2. Additionally, Pepper Content emphasized combining human expertise with AI. The team also ensured that the enterprise model was designed for scalability, enabling companies to produce content at scale without compromising quality.
3. They focused on customization where businesses could easily customize AI-generated content to reflect their unique brand voice, ensuring consistency across all marketing materials.

Although, this evolution to an enterprise model represented a significant milestone for them, this evolution wasn't linear. It was marked by a series of iterative steps, each guided by invaluable feedback from customers.

The Change Was Painful

But with the journey also came a lot of challenges. This shift also required them to restructure business operations, realign strategies and redefine the company's value proposition. It also meant building trust and credibility in a new market segment, which required time and effort.

Additionally, as Pepper Content aimed to position itself as an AI co-pilot for enterprise marketers, it faced the challenge of developing and integrating advanced technologies into its platform. This required significant investment in research and development and ensuring seamless integration with existing systems and workflows.

When an entrepreneur or a startup moves from the prototype to the later stages of MVP and of the product, the value proposition also sometimes needs to be moulded and tweaked. In tweaking, the value proposition gets clearer and refined. As they moved to an enterprise model, the platform's value proposition became clearer—to help businesses scale their content marketing efforts effectively. Today, Pepper's curated creators have created more than 1,00,000 content pieces through the platform, earning over $4,00,000 in creator fees. They have also served more than 2500 customers, including global firms like Amazon, Adobe and Google, and over 1,20,000 content creators, according to the company's website.[5]

With Anirudh's case study done and dusted, our chapter is not done yet. We still haven't answered practical questions like the cost of a prototype, where to fund the prototype, etc. Before you await with bated breath, let us jump into it right away.

Cost of a Prototype and Where to Find the Money For It?

The cost of physical prototypes can vary based on materials, components and labour. If your design is complex or you are using advanced production methods, prototyping is surely going to cost more.

To give you a context, a 3D printer can even cost you Rs 2.5 lakh and can go even higher depending upon material, complexity, processing and printing size. Similarly, a CNC machine for cutting cans start at Rs 30,000 and go till even Rs 5 lakh depending on the technology and axis.

Whether it's a simple click-through design or a near-functional app, the cost would depend on the level of detail and features you need to showcase your core value proposition. And as a startup, you probably don't have much money to just spend on validating your idea, so you need to be wise in evaluating how much is enough for showcasing your value proposition.

To address the question of financing, platforms like startupIndia.org list numerous institutions offering grants, mentorship (platforms like MAARG) and resources for early-stage startups. Not only do you get funding, but you also have the technical expertise and know-how to make your prototype commercially viable.

Prototyping is a patient, iterative process in which one needs to constantly test and refine until the core functionalities seamlessly blend with product features. As we also saw in the story of Pepper Content, a product is never truly final—it keeps evolving even when a business reaches significant milestones, say Rs 1000 crore in revenue.

Why? Because customer needs are constantly changing. Their preferences, priorities and expectations shift with changes in culture, technology and economic conditions. What works today might become irrelevant tomorrow. Hence, successful startups and businesses must stay nimble and adaptable, continuously updating their products to meet ever-evolving customer demands.

To sum up, prototyping is about patience, persistence and feedback. A product is never final and it's an evolving entity driven by customer needs.

Key Takeaways

- **Listening over Pitching:** Prioritize listening to customer problems over pitching your product.

- **Carefully Choose Channels:** Focus on perfecting selected distribution channels instead of spreading resources too thin.
- **Skip the Haste:** Avoid rushing to the next stage. As entrepreneurs, it's tempting to chase the next big thing, but take time to be calm, intentional, and reflective.
- **Opt for Functionality Over Design:** Don't obsess over perfecting the design. Optimize for functionality rather than beauty, especially in the early stages.

So, What Should You Do Next?

Go to an Atal Tinkering Lab by NITI Aayog in any designated school and list down any two prototypes you saw in the labs and the machines used to create them. You can find the list of schools at aim.gov.in.

Also, like in the previous chapter, given below is the framework called RISING, which will guide you through Pepper Content's journey in a nutshell:

Roadblock	**Ideal Customer**	**Solution**	**Innovation**	**Nakad (Money)**	**Growth**
Shifting from a content marketplace model to an enterprise-level product Managing the complexities of developing advanced technologies and integrating them into the platform Balancing the needs of content creators and enterprise clients	Small- to medium-sized businesses needing content creators for various projects Freelancers and creative professionals seeking work opportunities Large enterprises and businesses looking for a strategic partner to enhance their content marketing efforts	Content marketplace Developing an AI-powered platform that acts as a co-pilot for enterprise marketers Providing a comprehensive solution that includes content strategy, access to top-tier talent, and advanced technology to scale content creation	Integrating AI to automate and enhance content creation processes, making it more efficient for businesses to produce high-quality content at scale	Subscription or usage-based fees for enterprise clients leveraging the AI-powered platform and top-tier talent network	Pivoting to an enterprise model to cater to larger clients with more significant content needs Building a network of over 1,20,000 content creators and serving more than 2500 customers

4

Do I Need Technology?

The VC-Funded Startup Expand My Business

'Expand My Business'[1] *is India's first managed marketplace for B2B digital services. It is the largest digital services provider with more than thirty-six services in IT development, digital marketing, resource augmentation and blockchain technologies. They have a network of buyers across nineteen countries in the world and some of the industries and domains they work with are e-commerce, food and beverage, travel, healthcare and medical, real estate, gaming, transportation and more. Expand My Business is an end-to-end platform helping people discover the perfect vendor and the scope of work in addition to safeguarding payments through escrow solutions. Till date, they have raised $8.78 million in funding from leading marquee investors.*

In the last chapter, we explored how products are made, from the initial idea to the final creation. We also looked at a crucial part of this process called 'prototyping'. But the real question is: 'How do you actually go from creating that plan and then the prototype to actually creating the product?' The answer can be: technology.

In fact, there is a little bit of technology in everything that you do, eat or travel. Need to pay for your cab but do not have money? Pay through Paytm, GPay or any of these UPI apps. Feeling hungry at midnight? You order a burger through Zomato or Swiggy.

Kyun! Mooh mein paani aaya na? Is your mouth watering? Now, that is not technology.

And when it comes to urgent needs, such as an ambulance ride, services like Blinkit leverage technology to ensure help arrives quickly, even in the most critical moments.

However, technology is not just limited to these examples. It could be much more. Wayyyy more! Now, if you are as excited to know more as we were while adding those extra 'y's, stay with us and keep reading.

So, what is technology and what isn't? Does everything need to be 'technologized' or can things be done '*purane taur-tareeko se* [using old means and methods]'? And how do we utilize technology in its most optimum way?

With the rapid evolution of technology, the lines between its benefits and demerits are becoming increasingly blurred every single day. Therefore, it becomes crucial to delineate the boundaries of technology.

In the figure that follows, you can see that technology doesn't stand alone—it relies on and is connected to two crucial pillars: people and processes. The three together give rise to the intended product or service as denoted by the overlapping area.

The people involved are the ones who make the technology work. Whether we're using it or creating it, people are at the centre. It's about understanding what people need and working as a team to make technology useful and user-friendly. Processes are like a well-thought-out plan that helps use technology effectively. So, yes you do need technology!

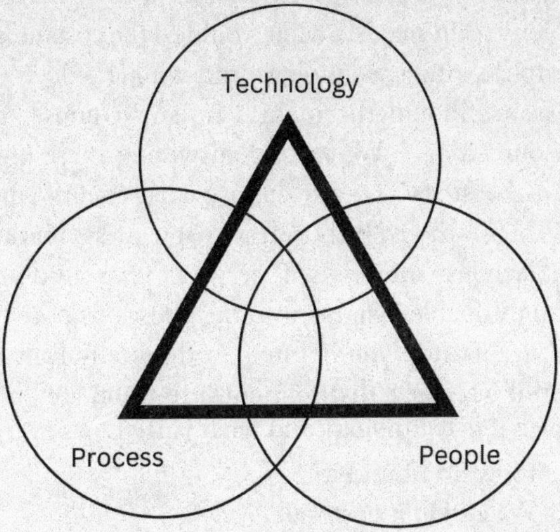

The Tech Triad

Now, answering the questions posed above, technology can be seen as two things. Firstly as an enabler and secondly as a core unit. When technology functions as an enabler, it facilitates and enhances the execution of various business processes and operations. In the case of Oyo, technology enables the core service of hotel discovery and booking. Here, technology isn't the primary product itself but the hotel is. On the other hand, when technology is the core product, it is a pure tech company. For instance, companies like TCS, Wipro and Infosys build their business around technology itself, providing core tech and software driven products.

As you navigate this chapter, you will learn the importance of technology to a startup, to what extent is technology really needed, what would be the costs associated with implementing technology and who should you get it made from. Should the makers be an in-house team or an outsourced one? We will be answering these questions through the story of two young entrepreneurs who have made it big in the B2B (business-to-business) marketplace space. Their experiences will serve as your guiding light, providing valuable insights into the questions posed above.

But let us stop you before you think any further. The next set of questions that may come to mind are:

- How do I build it?
- What will it cost me?
- At what scale should I start to get serious about it?
- Should I outsource it to a third-party vendor, or should I build my own technology team?
- Does technology always equate to success?

In this chapter, we will not only answer the above questions but also dive deeper into some case studies that will enable you with a better understanding of different kinds of scenarios and opportunities to integrate technology into your business.

Case study within a case study? Let's go!

From Corporate to Startup: The Journey of Building 'Expand My Business'

It would now be right to introduce Rohan, the co-founder of Expand My Business, to demystify the answers to the rest of the questions posed at the beginning of this section.

***Surya and Aditya:* 'Welcome Rohan. Thanks for coming here to share your insights for this book and for this crucial topic—tech or no tech. Can you share a bit of your journey with us and how it has been?'**

***Rohan:* 'Thanks for having me. Happy to share the insights that we have garnered through building Expand My Business.'**

Now, we thought of presenting this chapter through the exact conversation we had with Rohan. But for the sake of brevity and effectiveness, we will be presenting the story of Rohan and his co-founder Nishant through the case study format, which we have used in the other chapters as well.

The entrepreneurial journey of Rohan and Nishant began with an unlikely partnership. While Nishant had a background in consulting at PwC and Rohan had honed his skills at Adidas, their paths converged through shared experiences during their college days. They both pursued mechanical engineering at Vellore Institute of Technology (VIT) and collaborated on various projects during their college years. Both of them were involved in various cultural and tech fests and were also part of AIESEC[2] and Toastmasters[3] chapters. Fast forward to their post-college days, Nishant and Rohan found themselves in the same city, working in different industries.

With the bond that they had built during their engineering days, they decided to meet and discuss their entrepreneurial aspirations. Nishant had already established a successful business procuring handicrafts from tier-3 cities and selling them in Chandigarh. However, he faced challenges when trying to expand his business online. His experience exposed a gap in the market for procuring digital services. One day, when he was attempting to build his website, he faced the arduous task of finding a suitable vendor. He spent a significant amount of time, around forty-five days, searching for the right fit. Unfortunately, his quest led him to the wrong vendor, resulting in a loss of approximately Rs 50,000.

Such a huge loss when you are just starting out seems disastrous, doesn't it? But that loss gave birth to a sense of purpose. A purpose to streamline and expose millions of businesses and SMEs to the sheer power of having technology on their side. This purpose turned into Expand My Business. You see, entrepreneurs often find their inspiration in the problems and losses that they face within their industries. Their minds come pre-equipped with antennas that are always waiting to catch the next few signals of problems. Entrepreneurs often struggle to identify trustworthy and competent service providers from the myriad options available. This difficulty can lead to costly mistakes and wasted resources.

This predicament led to the birth of Expand My Business, a platform they designed to address these challenges.

Defining the All Important 'Vision'

The co-founders' vision for the business was not merely about creating another startup. It was rooted in a desire to revolutionize the way digital services were procured and delivered. Having faced problems themselves, they drew inspiration from the success story of Alibaba,[4] which had democratized manufacturing in China.

Rohan and Nishant always dreamt big. They envisioned creating a platform where businesses and SMEs could seamlessly access the services they needed for building and growing their own operations. Their goal was to streamline the process, eliminating the need to engage with multiple vendors and thereby reducing costs. They aimed to eradicate the common problem of trial and error for businesses and SMEs. They wanted to make this as easy as buying products from an e-commerce site.

Nothing But a Mission

Rohan and Nishant's initial foray was into crafting straightforward information websites. These served as the foundation upon which they ventured into creating a marketplace and a one-stop shop for services. What started with just a simple mission was soon serving over 2700 clients in the next three-and-a-half years, and that was just the beginning!

Adopting the 3D Approach

The Expand My Business platform focused on a 3D approach:

Discovery: Entrepreneurs often struggle to find reliable vendors in the crowded digital services market.

Decision: Even when potential vendors are identified, entrepreneurs lack sufficient information to make informed decisions based on factors like industry experience, budget compatibility and technology stack.

Delivery: Trust concerns arise due to the advanced payment model, with clients fearing unreliable vendors might vanish with their funds.

Now, do you remember the three questions we asked you? Even if you don't, let us pose them again:

- What will building a technology stack cost me?
- At what scale should I start to get serious about technology? Does technology always equate to success?
- Should I outsource it to a third-party vendor, or shall I build my own technology team?

Let's look at some real case studies from projects carried out by Expand My Business to answer each of the foregoing questions. These following case studies have been taken from the Expand My Business website.[5]

Case Study 1:

'What will building a technology stack cost me?'

Why Statement: Expand My Business collaborated with an emerging electronics brand to tackle challenges in establishing a robust digital presence and driving sales. With limited internal expertise and resources in e-commerce and online marketplace management, the brand sought assistance to navigate the competitive landscape effectively.

What Expand My Business Did: The team provided tailored marketplace-building services to address the specific needs of the electronics brand. This encompassed a range of crucial tasks including platform selection and setup, customized storefront design, product listing optimization and performance analytics and optimization. Each step was meticulously executed to ensure maximum effectiveness in enhancing the brand's online presence and driving sales.

Probable Cost: Potential cost components included platform setup fees, design and development expenses, investment in product listing optimization, analytics tools and ongoing maintenance costs.

Impact: Notable impacts included a 43 per cent increase in digital presence, a remarkable 57 per cent surge in sales volume within the initial three months and a substantial 38 per cent improvement in customer engagement metrics.

Key Learnings for Readers: There is no one-size-fits-all costing for services. The investment required for building a technology stack varies based on factors such as service scope, platform complexity and customization needs. Understanding these variables is crucial for businesses to make informed decisions and allocate resources effectively.

Case Study 2:

'At what scale should I start to get serious about technology? Does technology always equate to success?'

Why Statement: Expand My Business partnered with a dynamic tech startup based in Saudi Arabia to address challenges in establishing a robust digital presence and driving sales. The startup, renowned for its innovative solutions, aimed to leverage digital advertising to amplify its sales trajectory in the competitive information technology domain.

What Expand My Business Did: The company provided tailored digital marketing (advertising) services to meet the specific needs of the tech startup. It crafted targeted ad campaigns to reach the startup's ideal customer demographics, created engaging ad content to showcase its innovative solutions, continuously optimized campaigns based on real-time data and implemented a multifaceted approach across various digital advertising channels.

Impact: Notable impacts included a remarkable 57 per cent increase in sales revenue within the first quarter, a 63 per cent surge in website traffic and engagement and a 40 per cent boost in customer inquiries and conversions attributed to the ad campaigns.

Key Learnings for Readers:

1. **At What Scale Should I Start to Get Serious About Technology?** Whenever you have a core feature or product that can be easily monetized, you need to reach to your customers with the right offering. Then, build user-friendly tech and advertise your core offerings through the proper channels.
2. **Does Technology Always Equate to Success?** While technology can be a powerful tool for enhancing visibility and driving sales, success is not guaranteed solely by its adoption. Strategic planning, targeted marketing and continuous optimization are essential factors that contribute

to the effectiveness of technology in achieving business objectives. It's important to consider technology as part of a holistic approach to business growth rather than a standalone solution.

Case Study 3:

'Should I outsource my technology and service requirements to a third-party vendor, or shall I build my own team?'

Why Statement: A prominent travel brand sought to expedite the launch of four new verticals within a short timeframe while maintaining its commitment to exceptional service. Limited internal resources and expertise posed challenges to executing expansion plans effectively, necessitating the augmentation of their team with skilled professionals.

What Expand My Business Did: The team used its expertise in staff augmentation to address the travel brand's challenges. It conducted a comprehensive assessment of their staffing requirements, sourced skilled professionals with expertise in relevant tech stacks, provided dedicated project managers for coordination and offered continuous support and training to integrated staff members.

Impact:

1. Revenue Increase
2. Enhanced Operational Efficiency
3. Cost Saving

Key Learnings for Readers:

Should I Outsource or Build My Own Team?

Initially, outsourcing technology and service requirements to a third-party vendor, as demonstrated in this case study, can offer numerous advantages for businesses, especially when facing urgent requirements or skill gaps. By leveraging staff augmentation, companies can quickly access specialized expertise without the time and resources required for hiring and training a full-time team.

Furthermore, by entrusting specific tasks to external experts, you can concentrate your internal efforts and resources on core business functions, fostering innovation and strategic growth. However, it's important to recognize that outsourcing may not be a long-term solution for every aspect of business operations.

Moreover, having an in-house team provides greater control and customization over processes and outcomes, which may be essential for maintaining a competitive edge in the long run.

But how to build the in-house team?

When we were discussing the same question with the founders themselves, they jokingly said, and we quote, 'Sometimes, in order to attract the top tech-talent, you need to give them Jaguars, Audis and whatnot. It is damn expensive, especially for a new startup.'

It may require substantial upfront investments in recruitment, training and infrastructure. Either look to bootstrap, raise funding or even get a loan. The idea is to give as much incentive to the top tech talent as possible.

Another great hack is using ESOPs, which we will discuss later in the book.

Time to Wrap up!

To summarize, there is nothing better than building your own tech team. However, it is always better to outsource for core expertise in situations of human resource's (people) crunch. Later on, you always have the option to bring it inhouse as your business grows, and you get funding and the revenue too to hire top tech talent.

Key Takeaways

- **Avoid Fads:** Never introduce new technology for the sake of it. Analyze if you actually need it. Don't adopt the fad. Utilize your insights to make technology work for you. If you don't need it, don't use it.
- **Market Research Is Key:** Oftentimes, when starting a new business, we jump straight into product development without fully grasping our target audience's needs. Prioritize deep market research before anything else.
- **Stick to Core Values:** While technology is an enabler and enhances your product offering, never forget to stick to your core value proposition. Technology should amplify your mission, not distract from it.
- **Keep Evolving:** Technology evolves quickly and staying flexible and responsive to changes is key to long-term success.

So, What Should You Do Next?

Write down your five favourite applications and jot down reasons why they are your favourite. Perhaps you will get the answer to build your app similarly.

Also, like in the previous chapter, given below is the framework called RISING, which will guide you through Expand My Business's journey in a nutshell:

Roadblock	**Ideal Customer**	**Solution**	**Innovation**	**Nakad (Money)**	**Growth**
Difficulty in finding reliable vendors for digital services Nishant lost Rs 50,000 to an unreliable vendor after spending forty-five days searching for one	Small and medium-sized enterprises (SMEs) and startups Businesses lacking internal expertise and resources for digital services	End-to-end platform for discovering, selecting, and engaging digital service vendors	3D approach (Discovery, Decision, Delivery) for structured and reliable vendor engagement	Service fees and commissions	Positioned as a leader in the B2B digital services marketplace in India

5

Solo Date or Mentorship?

The Tale of a 100-Million-Dollar Startup Founder

tanX.fi,[1] *a crypto trading execution platform, founded by university friends Shaaran Lakshminarayanan (CEO), Bhavesh Praveen (CTO) and Ritumbhara Bhatnagar (Chief Design Officer), is an order book spot decentralized exchange (DEX) that aims to address the shortcomings being faced by crypto traders when trading. tanX.fi—previously tanX—is valued at $100 million as of today.*

While we were at the Leap Ahead startup summit in Chandigarh, the chief mentor and founder of PadUp Ventures, Pankaj Thakar, said 95 per cent of startups fail due to lack of mentors.

Now, what comes to your mind when you hear the word 'mentor'? Teacher? Guide? Advisor? Whatever does, mentors certainly are more than just the term, which itself embodies a blend of roles and attributes.

As per the Oxford Dictionary, a mentor is an experienced person, who advises and helps somebody with less experience over a period of time.[2]

In Bharat's sanskriti [Indian culture], the guru–shishya parampara [teacher–disciple tradition] has been upheld since times immemorial. The roots of this tradition can be traced back to the ancient Vedic times, when knowledge was transmitted orally from guru to shishya in gurukuls [traditional schools]. The guru not only imparted academic knowledge but also instilled moral values, spiritual insights and practical skills necessary for leading a fulfilling life.

Understanding this guru–shishya parampara still holds relevance in today's world and age of startups.

Who Is a Mentor? And Why Do You Need One?

A guru for a startup can be the mentor(s) who offer valuable insights acquired from either their own entrepreneurial journey, or from advising and guiding numerous entrepreneurs across various industries.

They can provide guidance regarding each phase of the entrepreneurial journey, the fifteen phases that we have also mentioned in this book (Refer to the table of contents: the fifteen chapters cover a different phase of entrepreneurship each).

Let's say you are trying to raise funds for your startup but don't understand how term sheets work. That's where a mentor who has been through multiple fundraising rounds can guide you. Now, there are numerous reasons why you would need a mentor in your startup journey.

A few of them are mentioned below:

1. **A mentor can help you refine your go-to-market strategy.**
2. **A mentor can connect you to the right vendors, distributors, investors, etc.**
3. **The 'right' mentor also becomes a sounding board to bounce off various ideas and strategies.**
4. **A good mentor also helps you in your lowest tide and encourages you to keep marching.**

Whenever one hears the term 'mentor', they often think of someone senior, but the 'right' mentor can in fact be anyone. It can be your friend, a colleague or even books. Yes, mentors can be amorphous too as we will also see through the journey of the entrepreneur in this chapter. Finding the right mentor is very important. Compatibility is key and can't be ignored. However, a mentor–mentee relationship doesn't always have to be perfect.

Now, How Do You Know that You Have Found the 'Right Mentor'?

Don't worry just yet, we will be guiding you through our protagonist, who underwent the journey of finding the 'right mentor' while building something really big in the crypto and DeFi space. In this chapter, we embark on a journey through the experiences of Shaaran Lakshminarayanan, Bhavesh Praveen and Ritumbhara Bhatnagar, the co-founders of tanX.fi, as they navigate the often intricate process of finding the right mentor and assembling a cohesive team to build a company valued at 100 million dollars today.

Now, when we were interviewing the founders of tanX, we found out that these people were still in college when they started. But that's not it! Shaaran, one of the co-founders and the person we interviewed for this chapter, told us that he started building things when he was just in his pre-teen years. He also participated in hackathons and whatnot, winning quite a few of them!

There's a specific reason why we chose Sharaan and tanX.fi for this chapter—he has a very 'special' mentor. In fact, it's not even someone who's human—wait, what?!

Let's learn more through his story!

tanX's Journey and 'Special' Mentor

Shaaran emphasized the importance of industry connections. Transitioning from cybersecurity and crypto to tanX, these connections were invaluable for him and his team. While he credited various mentors, he also highlighted that much of his learning came from documentation (the official written materials that provide detailed information and guidance on a specific technology, framework or system, including user manuals, installation guides, API references, whitepapers and technical specifications) rather than traditional resources like YouTube or courses.

Yes, Sharaan's mentors are his books. Knowledge itself has been his guide—like an amorphous mentor, shaping his perspective in ways that conventional mentors often don't. But it is not that he has not learned from humans. He also learned from pioneers in the ecosystem, such as the CEOs of StarkWare, Uri Kolodny and Eli Ben-Sasson, and Sandeep Nailwal from Polygon. These mentors provided unconventional insights and research support, crucial for solving complex problems.

Shaaran also mentioned that he preferred reading research papers (a special mentor) and code to understand and solve problems. For example, StarkWare's engineering team provided extensive support to tanX. They helped by offering in-depth technical guidance and conducting comprehensive research sessions. This collaboration enabled tanX to optimize their systems and address complex issues effectively. Having such expertise outside their internal team significantly boosted their capabilities and contributed to their rapid developmental success.

Challenges Faced by Young and First-Time Founders

While the challenges faced by young and first-time founders are immense, the common grey areas are market research and problem identification. They also sometimes overestimate their understanding of the problems they're tackling.

These founders compile a list of problems to solve, but they often get carried away by glamorous or fancy ones because '*basic problems se unhe kick nahi milti* [they don't get a kick out of basic problems]'. Consequently, they plunge into developing solutions without fully grasping and understanding the nuances of their target market. This situation is like digging a well only to find no water!

Now, Shaaran with his years of experience in the crypto space, along with his co-founders and team at tanX, was able to decrypt a critical need for decentralized trading solutions tailored for high-frequency traders. This deep familiarity allowed them to perceive trends and anticipate emerging needs much before their counterparts and that too with clarity. As Sam Bankman-Fried's FTX collapse sent shockwaves through the crypto world, the team at tanX recognized this event as more than a momentary disruption and positioned the platform to capitalize on the shifting preferences of traders accordingly.

Despite the relatively young team at tanX, they were still able to recognize the need for guidance and senior leadership to navigate the rapidly evolving decentralized finance (DeFi) landscape. To address this, tanX strategically hired experienced professionals from established companies like Flipkart and WazirX to bolster their ranks.

As they say, 'It only takes one man to move a needle, but it takes many to move mountains.' The team at tanX needed solid mentors, who could guide them through the complexities of the crypto market, ensuring they could effectively implement their vision and adapt to the challenges posed by a competitive environment.

For this, they decided to assemble the right team, as mentioned above, at both senior and junior levels.

But how did Shaaran and his team do just that? Let us find out.

Assembling the Right Team: How to Make the Next Set of Hires Apart from Your Core Team?

Building a successful venture requires assembling a team that aligns with your vision, values and objectives. As you move beyond your core team, strategic hiring becomes paramount to sustain growth and innovation. One of the most crucial aspects of making hiring decisions is to prioritize cultural fits over skill fits. Sure, skills and experience are vital, but they're only part of the puzzle. Think of it like fitting puzzle pieces together—if they don't match, the picture won't look right. Hence, cultural fit matters a lot—more than skills fit, because skills can be taught, but culture needs to be ingrained in our hearts and minds.

Now, during our interview, Shaaran mentioned a few key pointers with regards to building a solid hiring framework. They are:

1. **Internal Recruitment Focus:** Prioritizing internal referrals and networking over external agencies promotes trust and unity within the team.
2. **Strategic Leadership Recruitment**: A meticulous approach to hiring leaders involves engaging investors, internal referrals and personal connections to ensure organizational fit.
3. **Cultural Alignment**: Understanding how leadership roles influence company culture is vital. Assessing candidates' alignment with the company's vision and values is key.

4. **Embracing Age Diversity**: Advocating for a balanced age demographic within the team fosters diverse perspectives, driving innovation and cultural cohesion.
5. **Vision Alignment**: Ensuring leadership aligns with the organizational vision requires open dialogue and transparent communication to establish mutual expectations.
6. **Adapt, Improve, Build**: Emphasizing ongoing evaluation and adaptation in the recruitment process allows for learning from mistakes and refining strategies to meet evolving organizational needs.

Having turned through the pages of this chapter, now that you understand the importance of finding the right mentor—and that anyone can be your mentor—you might be wondering: 'Why would someone even become my mentor? Why would people root for me? Do I have to offer them something in return?'

Well, just read on.

How to Compensate Your Mentor? The Guru Dakshina

While compensation can take different forms, it's important to understand that not all mentors expect something in return. Many genuinely believe in your potential and are willing to root for you simply because they want to help.

That said, when it's appropriate, here are some effective ways to compensate a mentor:

1. **Equity**: Offering a small percentage of equity in your business can be a powerful way to compensate a mentor. This not only acknowledges their valuable contributions but also aligns their interests with the success of your venture. Ensure this arrangement is clearly outlined and legally documented.
2. **Reciprocal Mentorship**: If you possess expertise in an area your mentor might find valuable, offer to provide guidance or support in that domain. This reciprocal relationship can foster mutual growth and respect.
3. **Financial Compensation**: Depending on the nature and extent of the mentorship, consider offering financial compensation. This could be in the form of a monthly stipend, a consulting fee or payment for specific sessions.

Conclusion: Learning Is Everywhere and So Is the Right Mentor!

The right mentor is the one who provides you with the guidance, support and wisdom to help you grow and succeed. It is never a boss–employee relationship where the goal is to show authority. It is a student–teacher relationship where the goal is mutual learning and growth. In fact, a mentor learns a lot, too, with the founder's journey and real-time experiences.

Since mentorship is not a classroom lesson, it doesn't come packaged as a formal session. It lies in everyday insights, real-time problem-solving and the casual yet valuable conversations that leave you thinking differently. Mentorship can happen in the flow of work as well, where experience meets execution.

We are not saying you need a mentor—that's entirely your decision. What we are saying is that learning should never stop. Whether through a mentor's guidance, real-world experiences, or even in the people you hire (like in Shaaran and his team's case), the key is to stay open, curious and constantly evolving. After all, in the ever-changing landscape of entrepreneurship, continuous learning is your greatest asset.

So, wake up and seek your guru. For *guru bin gyaan nahin* [there is no knowledge without a teacher/mentor].

Guru Govind dou khade, kaake laagun paaye,
Balihaari guru aap ne, Govind diyo milaye.

When Guru and God stand before me,
to whom should I pay my respects first?
Indeed it is my teacher, who has shown
me the path to my God.

Key Takeaways

- **Overcoming Challenges:** When just starting up, first-time founders often face challenges regarding mentorship, such as asking for help, uncertainty about how to approach potential mentors, lack of clarity on goals and difficulty in building connections. For this, one should take proactive steps, like reframing their mindset about asking for help, preparing thoughtful outreach messages (more on this in Chapter 14), defining clear mentorship goals and actively seeking networking opportunities.

- **Find Your Mentor in Anything:** Never think that a mentor can only be a person. It can also be a document, a video or any other resource that provides guidance and insight, as we saw in Shaaran's journey. Embracing diverse forms of mentorship can significantly enhance your learning experience and provide valuable perspectives on your entrepreneurial path.
- **Seek Mentorship Actively:** Just go out there and seek mentorship opportunities actively. Don't be afraid! You will never know what lies in store for you if you don't even try.

So, What Should You Do Next?

List down five things you have learnt from your parents and how they have helped you to grow in life.

Also, like in the previous chapter, given below is the framework called RISING, which will guide you through tanX's journey in a nutshell:

Roadblock	**Ideal Customer**	**Solution**	**Innovation**	**Nakad (Money)**	**Growth**
Balancing academic responsibilities with managing crises and engaging with various stakeholders Coordination among different parties, including banks, customers and law enforcement agencies to address financial and security concerns	High-frequency crypto traders	Decentralized platform, where one can trade from their Fireblocks account or any wallet without having to compromise on fees, swiftness, experience and liquidity	Back-end support for centralized exchanges and hedge funds, optimizing liquidity management	Comissions on transactions	Actively building by seeking mentorship from industry experts and hiring them .

6

Right Team, Culture and ESOPs

Odyssey of GrowthSchool

GrowthSchool[1] *is a community-led live learning platform. They aim to fill the gap between industry requirements and the existing academic curriculum through community-led cohort programmes. These are curated to teach skills that are relevant on the job in a short period, so that students become employable immediately. Their aim is to partner with the top 1 per cent of instructors to create high-impact cohort-based courses on personal and professional growth. To date, they have raised a total of $5 million from prominent investors like Nikhil Kamath, Peak XV (erstwhile Sequoia Capital India & SEA) and more. They were also a part of the coveted LinkedIn Top Indian Startup list in 2022 and 2023.*

At this point of the book, you would have already learnt about some basic startup terms such as ideation and finding the right problem to solve, choosing the right startup idea, creating the first prototype of the product or service and whether to outsource tech or to insource it.

But all this doesn't come without building a team—a solid army of people who believe in you and your soon-to-be company's vision.

Napoleon the Great had quoted, 'Great ambition is the passion of a great character.' Well, the extension of this quote is also true to startups. 'Great startups are the passion of a great team.'

We can't emphasize enough how building a great team in most cases is paramount to a startup's success. But more crucial than building a team is retaining it—retaining the core set of people who live and breathe your mission. Although it is also important to retain the high-performing members who join your team later, it is all the more important to retain those initial members—those who were there when you were nothing, in fact had nothing. They have seen the tough times and in most cases are willing to start from ground zero, if needed. They are willing to go back to square one.

Have you seen the OTT startup Stage's pitch on Shark Tank India? Even if not, let us tell you that their earlier venture, WittyFeed, closed down overnight—and yet more than 80 per cent of their team stayed back and decided to rebuild a new venture altogether.

Yes! You need members who, if needed, are willing to rework on a new business altogether.

Finding these 'foundation members' is hard. They may come at a cost that you can't afford at that initial stage, when you have no revenue or funding. Funding will come in when the investors are convinced of a strong team. Also, these required team members may not be available in the same place and convincing them to shift base to the place of your startup may not be easy in terms of the compensation they may demand. Even if they do get convinced, the next problem will be to actually bring them together into a cohesive team, who believe in the vision and the potential of your startup.

But the question arises—how the hell do you keep these good people on your side? How do you retain them?

There are many ways of retaining important members and talent. One such way that we will be focusing on in this chapter is ESOPs.

An ESOP stands for an employee stock ownership plan that enables employees to own a part of the company they work for. These ESOPs act as a 'loyalty builder', with companies typically setting aside a 10–15 per cent pool of shares to be allocated to team members. When your team owns a piece of the pie, their interests naturally start aligning with the company's goals. This can further translate into heightened motivation, unwavering commitment and a shared sense of purpose.

ESOPs also offer other benefits such tax advantages and serve as a catalyst for attracting and retaining top talent. In short, ESOPs are a win-win as they do both—foster and keep employee satisfaction in check and drive the startup's growth. As per Inc42, twenty-three startups undertook buyback schemes, which helped 3000-plus employees generate wealth worth more than Rs 1,448 crore.[2] In 2023, ESOP buybacks by a mere twelve startups helped their employees net $850 million, albeit $700 million came from Flipkart alone.[3]

At this point, let us tell you that even Ritesh Agarwal, founder of OYO Rooms, faced the same challenge of retention initially, which he overcame by the use of the retention tool called ESOPs.[4] When Ritesh was in the initial few years of starting OYO, known as Oravel Stays Limited at the time, he met Anuj Tejpal, an IIT graduate who had just returned from the US. Anuj was so impressed with Ritesh and his idea that he wanted to work with him to build Oravel into what would eventually become OYO. Ritesh liked Anuj, but at the time, he didn't have any money to offer. So, he asked Anuj how they could even make it work. Ritesh was quite shocked at the fact that an IIT graduate was so eager to work with him. Anuj said, 'Arre yaar, we'll figure out something with ESOPs. Don't worry about the salary; just give me ESOPs.' Ritesh was hearing about ESOPs for the first time, but soon realized they were a powerful retention tool for the people he would hire next as well.

Now, that we have presented you with an overview of why and how of ESOPs, let's look at a few basic terms related to them. Don't get overwhelmed by trying to fully understand every detail. Just get acquainted with the key terms. Here are a couple of important ones:

- **Vesting**: Vesting refers to the process by which employees earn ownership of their ESOPs over time. Rather than receiving all their shares immediately, they earn them gradually based on their tenure at the company.

On or after January 1, 2025	500 Equity Shares (10%)
On or after January 1, 2026	1,000 Equity Shares (20%)
On or after January 1, 2027	1,500 Equity Shares (30%)
On or after January 1, 2028	2,000 Equity Shares (40%)

- **Accelerated Vesting:** Accelerated vesting allows employees to speed up earning their ESOPs, usually under specific circumstances like a merger, acquisition or company sale. Instead of waiting for the standard vesting period, employees can gain immediate ownership of their unvested shares, giving them a quick reward if the company undergoes a significant event. For example, in the above figure, there's 20 per cent vesting in Year 1, 30 per cent in Year 2 and so on.
- **Cliff Period**: The cliff period is the initial waiting period before employees start vesting in their ESOPs. Typically, this period lasts one year, after which the employee becomes eligible to receive their first portion of shares.
- **Buyback**: Buyback is a corporate action where a company can buy back the ESOPs from the employees. This allows employees to cash out their ESOPs. This typically happens on the four- or five-year anniversary from the date of issuance.

Now, for the purpose of making this concept of ESOPs as a retention tool clearer and also shedding light on other factors that come along with it, like team building and building a company culture, we interviewed the founder of GrowthSchool, Vaibhav Sisinty.

Vaibhav's Story of Courage, Resilience and Determination

Vaibhav, a first-year engineering student, was determined to make his own money. For this, he learnt to build websites. He built one about Android, called Discovering Android. This website ended up being his first startup at the age of nineteen. Having built a website, he also needed some visitors. So, he started learning about website fundamentals and SEO—in just three months, he was able to attract traffic to his website that was near to 1,00,000 visits per month. Through this, he was able to generate a profit of Rs 25,000. But soon, in the fourth month of its operation, Google banned the website due to some issues and discoveringandroid.com was no longer around. But as they say, failure doesn't come without its teachings. Having gone through the process of running a startup for three months, Vaibhav was already able to learn the crucial skills of building websites and marketing. However, he knew that these learnings were not enough for the long run and that he needed to upskill further. For the next seven to eight months, he invested his time in acquiring some more skills.

Soon, he entered the second year of engineering. At this time, he was determined to start something again, taking with him the lessons he learnt from building Discovering Android. He teamed up with three of his friends and built another company, called CrazyHeads, a digital media agency. The company aimed at providing website development and other digital design services for small companies and individuals. With a mission of promoting their company, they decided to conduct a huge ethical hacking workshop in their college. But they lacked the funds to actually execute the plan. Nevertheless, Vaibhav and the team were so determined that they applied their great marketing skills and managed to sell 450 tickets to the workshop in two months, each worth Rs 1000. But, as the date to the workshop was nearing, something turned the tide for them. Just three days before the event, all the colleges shut down due to a massive political event. Yet, this didn't stop them from conducting their event. In fact, they were able to attract more people than they expected—a whopping 750 attendees in the audience, which made the workshop, and their event, a huge success.

Now, imagine yourself getting huge success after a long journey full of struggles and challenges. Wouldn't you feel confident and want to replicate the success? You would, right?

After this unreal accomplishment, even Vaibhav and his friends felt extremely confident of their skills and thought that they would be able to attract clients by showcasing their work. They thought that everyone would want them—now that they had already overdelivered on their expectations, much like Shah Rukh Khan, whom people absolutely love and adore. But the bubble burst and what they were expecting didn't happen at all!

Fortunately, this didn't deter Vaibhav. He started to work for free for six months, before someone recognized his unending potential. Slowly but steadily, clients started coming in and in the next eighteen months, he worked with over 100 clients. Vaibhav managed to clear his education loan before even finishing college! CrazyHeads finally got recognized when it won the award for Fast Emerging Digital Media Startup of the year.

Now, money no longer remained Vaibhav's sole incentive and things that could act as motivations for him widened. Learning, growth and impact also became one of his core set of incentives. After building CrazyHeads for around three years, Vaibhav realized that he couldn't reach his full potential there, so he decided to take an exit from the company that he had built. In the following months and years, Vaibhav took on the next challenge. Soon, destiny found him at Uber, where he joined as a city coordinator. In just one-and-a-half years, was promoted to marketing manager at Uber. There, he got to work with people from top colleges like the IITs, which made him realize that the prestige of one's university doesn't really play a part in where life takes you next. After a stint of four-and-a-half years at Uber Hyderabad, Vaibhav got the opportunity to move to Mexico City. Everything had been organized, from selling his house in Hyderabad to renting a house in Mexico. However, just one day before that move, his relocation got cancelled and he decided to leave Uber.

Vaibhav then started working for an old startup called Klook as the marketing manager. Just before the second wave of Covid-19 began in September 2020, he lost his job.

Crashes! Crashes! Crashes! What else do you expect in the life of an entrepreneur?

If it would have been that easy, everyone would have done it and succeeded. But what people don't know about start ups is the constant hustle and frustration that one needs to make peace with. As statistics suggest, most startups fail at the ideation phase. Getting funded is talk of the distant future.

In startups, there are more thorns than roses.

As Vaibhav lost his job, don't you think he must have been shattered? So, how did he rise back despite all these challenges?

For this we need to delve further.

Revolutionizing How Young Professionals and Graduates Learn: Vaibhav's Second Innings and the Story of GrowthSchool

Vaibhav had started using LinkedIn in college itself as he had already decided to become an entrepreneur. His profile had quite a consistent growth in followers. So, he decided to try building something on top of this. Something that he had already done before—building his own personal brand and community on LinkedIn. He pilot-launched an online course on 'LinkedIn Growth', which turned out to be a great success. In addition, he also started to consult different brands for growth hacking, which is a subfield of marketing focused on the rapid growth of a company. The workshop went so well that soon, he had to launch multiple batches and finally, this turned into GrowthSchool. At this point, one of the attendees of his first batch, Uttam reached out to Vaibhav, asking if he needed any help with building this venture. Vaibhav liked his determination and decided to work with him to build GrowthSchool together. They deliberated, discussed and worked on identifying what they could offer for months. Their mission was simple—to take online courses, expand their width and involve various experts from different industries to create workshops that help the youth of the country get to the next level, upskilling them and making them industry-ready. Today, Both Vaibhav and Uttam spent hours building the core architecture, which eventually led them to building a team of rockstars and launching courses and masterclasses on numerous domains like AI, ChatGPT, search engine optimization (SEO), copywriting, UI/UX design, Google ads, Facebook ads marketing, direct-to-consumer (D2C) and whatnot!

As GrowthSchool started gaining a lot of user interest for their courses, they needed to build a team. A team that could help manage operations, marketing and sales, finance, human resources and anything that could help GrowthSchool scale upwards.

While today, GrowthSchool's team comprises 120 members, they had to develop a solid incentive plan to help grow and make that team stick. In other words, they had to build the right team with the right set of ingredients.

But the question is how does one build the right team and also retain them?

Remember we discussed ESOPs as a retention tool? GrowthSchool did the same, they created an ESOP pool and allocated ESOPs firstly to key members and then to individuals with substantial effect on the company's development and prosperity, such as pioneers who were taking many chances initially, key contributors responsible for innovations/business expansions, etc.

Yes ESOPs must remain exclusive to certain key members, otherwise their value may diminish. Nobody will be motivated to contribute to their best abilities, if everyone on the roster gets ESOPs.

Now if you are someone who has participated in their school/college clubs or tried building a team at your startup/workplace, you will agree with us that building a team is not easy.

Netflix, which is one of the most popular streaming entertainment platforms ever, owes a lot to this 'team building culture' by its founder Reed Hastings. This culture did not develop overnight but was rather developed through several deliberate practices and principles. We thought sharing some key lessons from the Netflix[5] story would serve as a great primer to building culture and teams at your own current startup or at your future startups.

Always Encourage High Performance

Netflix co-founder, Reed Hastings, envisioned an organization where excellence became a norm. He implemented a strict recruitment process to ensure that only the best talents joined the team.

Always Foster Transparency

Transparency is very important in creating trust as well as encouraging collaboration efforts between employees.

Be Innovative and Make that Innovation in line with your Startup's Goals

Countless number of times, teams at startups strive for innovation. But they don't so in the right direction. There is a misalignment between their innovation goals and what the startup would like to seek out from them.

Encourage Independence

While building a team, it is important to give your team members some space. One shouldn't just micromanage and should promote accountability and high levels of performance.

The Keeper Test

If a person said they were leaving for another job, you ask yourself if you would fight to keep them. If you wouldn't, you should consider firing them.

Promote Personal Growth

As a leader of your startup's pack, your job is to allow personal as well as professional growth. Your startup should put effort towards training and development of the workforce while also rewarding outstanding contributions and achievements, hence motivating your team to do more than their best.

How Do These ESOPs Contribute to Team Retention and When to Allocate Them? Now, imagine you have a great idea but not much else to offer—no fancy perks, no big salary. How do you convince an experienced professional to join your startup? As we saw in Ritesh's example, ESOPs are a powerful tool to do this. The reasons why that is the case are given below:

Fosters a Sense of Camaraderie and Mutual Support: As co-owners, team members understand that helping a colleague succeed directly benefits them. This sense of camaraderie and mutual support helps strengthen interpersonal relationships among the members and also helps build a cohesive and dynamic team.

Promotes Transparency: ESOPs increase the transparency concerning the financial status of the startup and its prospects. This consequently results in trust enhancement and improved team communication as now everybody has the relevant information.

Long-Term Wealth Building: Members view long-term financial gains through stock ownership as an incentive to remain with the startup.

Deferred Payouts: Vesting periods restrict the ESOPs to be exercised only after the members have completed a certain number of months or years at the startup. This makes members more driven to give in their all.

One more thing, always ensure the ESOP pool is created before funding. Having the pool established prior to funding rounds can prevent complications during future investments. If founders delay creating the ESOP until after securing investment, it may lead to further dilution issues and extended negotiations, complicating the entire investment process. After funding, the founder's equity gets diluted, and you will have fewer shares to offer to your team. By creating the pool beforehand, you can set aside the necessary equity for attracting and retaining key talent without sacrificing your stake in the company.

Given that ESOPs Are a Great Tool, Should You Allocate Them to Everyone Who Joins Your Startup?

The short answer is: No! When it comes to deciding who gets ESOP incentives, companies really need to take a closer look at their team. Giving stock options to all new members is not a good way of allocating them. ESOPs should be used strategically to entice top talents, most especially in early stages, when cash flows are tight and risks for the startup are huge. By making it possible for every member to have ESOPs, their value can decrease, and they will no longer be useful as a retention tool.

But ESOPs alone are not enough. You need more—that is, a great market potential that excites them about the future. If your idea targets a large, growing market, it signals high upside potential, which is crucial for attracting senior talent. Beyond that, experienced professionals seek an opportunity where they can create a direct impact. Show them how their expertise will shape the company's growth, whether it's in building a product, scaling operations or opening new markets.

Key Takeaways

- **Keep Motivating Your Team:** Build a team that thrives on internal motivation, not just external rewards. External incentives can fade, but internal motivation can be reignited and sustained over time.
- **ESOPs are a retention tool, but factors like work culture also play a crucial role:** Don't just rely on

ESOPs to retain people because if the work culture is toxic, even ESOPs won't help.

- **Learning Should Never Stop:** Ensure your team understands the 'why' behind their work. Create an environment where learning is valued and encouraged. A team that is always learning and growing will remain adaptable and innovative.
- **Give Your Team the Freedom to Take Ownership:** Give your team members the autonomy to make decisions and take ownership of their projects.
- **Embed 'Collaboration' in Your Cultural DNA:** Build a culture where collaboration is the norm, not the exception.
- **Recognition Is Key:** Regularly acknowledge the hard work and contributions of your team. Recognition not only boosts morale but also reinforces the behaviours you want to see repeated.

So, What Should You Do Next?

Study the ESOP Policy of companies which have given ESOP buybacks this year. And write three things that you find common across them.

Also, like in the previous chapter, given below is the framework called RISING, which will guide you through GrowthSchool's journey in a nutshell:

Roadblock	**Ideal Customer**	**Solution**	**Innovation**	**Nakad (Money)**	**Growth**
Not being able to decide which courses to run and shut	Young professionals and students seeking to upskill and advance their careers to become top 1 per cent	High-quality online courses and masterclasses	Involving industry experts to conduct workshops and masterclasses	Expanding variety of courses and consistent user interest contribute to sustainable financial growth	Strong focus on feedback and quality through metrics such as CSAT (customer satisfaction) to measure student happiness

7

Register in India Versus Outside

Crest's Homecoming to India

Crest[1] is a SaaS (software-as-a-service) startup that helps D2Cs (direct-to-consumer brands) and SMBs (small and medium businesses) accelerate revenue growth by eliminating frequent stock-outs. Launched in March 2022 by Rahul Vishwakarma, Akhil Kumar and Yogesh Byahatti, Crest seeks to assist brands in maintaining their financial stability by implementing efficient inventory practices to optimize their working capital. Some of Crest's clients are leading startups and brands such as Pilgrim, Whole Truth Foods and Wow Skin Science. Crest is backed by investors like July Ventures, IAN (Indian Angel Network), IPV (Inflection Point Ventures), FAAD Capital, and other prominent investors.

While the US is often seen as the Mecca of startups, offering a mature ecosystem, access to abundant venture capital and a vast market ready for innovative solutions, it comes with fierce competition and higher operational costs.

On the other hand, India is a rising star in the startup landscape. With its massive consumer base, lower operating costs and a burgeoning tech ecosystem, it presents a compelling option.

As per ZenBusiness,[2] a digital business services platform, the average duration from founding a startup to attaining unicorn status is now seven years, six months and twenty-five days in India. Meanwhile, for new-age companies based in the US, the journey takes seven years, three months and thirteen days.

In the past, it used to take much longer for startups in India to reach unicorn status compared to those in the US. However, recent trends show that these durations have now come much closer. This change indicates that India's startup scene has matured, becoming more efficient in fostering quick growth and innovation, much like the well-established startup environment in the US.

And it is just the beginning. *Picture toh abhi baki hai mere dost . . .*

At least 115 unicorns, presenting a combined valuation of USD 350 billion, and 1,47,846 startups are recognized by the DPIIT (Department for Promotion of Industry and Internal Trade) across 763 districts of the country. That is the sheer expanse of the Indian entrepreneurial ecosystem. With the third largest startup ecosystem in the world, Bharat also ranks second in innovation quality, with top positions in the quality of scientific publications and its universities among middle-income economies.[3]

These statistics tell us a lot about the rapidly expanding innovation prowess of Bharat. Furthermore, this innovation is not just limited to certain sectors, but rather is well spread out. Startups in Bharat are addressing unique problems across fifty-six diverse industrial sectors. For example, 13 per cent are within IT services, 9 per cent in healthcare and life sciences, 7 per cent in education, 5 per cent in agriculture, and 5 per cent in food and beverages.[4] Additionally, new and modern spaces such as AI and drone delivery are seeing a surge in entrepreneurial activity. From traditional industries to cutting-edge technologies, the spread of innovation in Bharat has never been so rapid and pervasive.

With these encouraging and eye-opening numbers about startups in India, there is one very important aspect and legal requirement for running a startup that should be discussed. It's the registration of a startup. This is a mandatory requirement in any country, without which many legal and financial problems may occur later.

Registering your startup is essential and mandated by law, but deciding *to* register is just 50 per cent of the process. The other 50 per cent lies in figuring out *where* to register. Yes, the location of registration is one aspect that needs to be considered before beginning the process. This is important because some places offer more benefits than others. For example, within India, some states have their own policies and benefits for registering in-house. Registering in another country is also an option. Sometimes, the requisite tech talent is available only outside. Also, in some cases, the product or service adoption is outside the country, especially in enterprise-level products.

This choice of location is usually influenced by certain parameters. These include:

1. **Legal and Regulatory Environment**
   This varies from place to place. Different locations have different rules. Some are more business-friendly, some have lower taxes and some have minimal essential paperwork. For example, there is a 100 per cent income tax exemption on export income for SEZ (Special Economic Zone) units under the Income Tax (I-T) Act for the first five years. This exemption may incentivize certain kinds of startups and business to register in an SEZ. Even Dubai for that matter offers tax benefits and investor-friendly policies that make it an attractive startup registration destination.
2. **Access to Funding**
   Some locations, especially the big cities or bustling tech hubs, have more investors. Think Bengaluru or Delhi in India. As per Inc42 Media, while Bengaluru reigns supreme as the top funded startup hub in Q1 of 2024, with a total of USD 853 million raised, Delhi clinches the second spot with a total of USD 441 million invested in.[5] So having a startup in such locations increases the probability of finding investors.
3. **Access to Talent and Resources**
   The registration should be done keeping an ideal combination of availability of talent and resources

and ease of registration, in mind. It may be that the talent or resources are available in one place and registration benefits in another.

4. **Proximity to Customers**
   Being close (proximity) to customers enables quicker response times to their needs. Also, access to customers in and around you can help to understand local market dynamics, customer preferences, pain points and their needs.
5. **Cost and Ease of Doing Business**
   Some locations offer incentives, grants and support programmes specifically designed to assist startups and small businesses. These programmes reduce the cost of starting and scaling a business.

The above list of parameters regarding registration of startups is not exhaustive. There could be other subtle factors that impact the decision regarding registration. Regardless of all the benefits available elsewhere, there will always be startups that choose to register their companies in their hometowns, and that's completely understandable. The sentimental value of staying close to one's roots is significant for many entrepreneurs.

But remember that the registration of a company shouldn't just be based on sentimental aspects. One should weigh in on the practical aspects of this decision. After all, you can't be emotional in business. You need to mind your business when doing business.

Why Do Some Startups Choose to Register Abroad?

In recent times, there has been a trend of establishing startups in other countries which is driven by certain factors, including attractive incentives and offers on provision of space, lower or no taxes, minimal risks, insurance against losses and easily available funding. To further understand this aspect in detail, we need to delve into the root of the issue.

Now, while we would be talking about the US whilst mentioning the scenario of establishing a startup abroad, there are other countries that have also been witnessing a rise in registrations of startups by Indian founders. Today, there are other countries such as Singapore, UAE and Malta, that are witnessing a positive impact as top startup registration destinations after the pandemic.

In a study[6] done by Ilya Strebulaev, a professor of finance at the Stanford Graduate School of Business, it was revealed that out of 1078 founders across 500 US unicorns, ninety were born in India.

This study also discovered that the majority of Indian founders were immigrants rather than US-born. The Indian founders constitute 8 per cent of all US unicorn founders, thus making them the second-most represented nationality after Americans.[7]

As per Aditya's experience of investing in more than 100 startups at FAAD Capital—'It is a common misconception in the startup community and even the general public that companies registered outside India are not Bharat-first companies, and that they are contributing to the development of foreign countries, draining talent and funds away from India. This is not the case.' Everything should not be observed under the lens of nationalism and patriotism. Business is business and it knows no boundaries. Progress of an Indian startup anywhere in the world contributes to the success of India and etches Bharat distinctly on the world's startup scenario.

Despite attractive or compelling reasons to register a startup abroad, the winds have started changing directions. Recently, startups that once chose to register in other countries have started the process of shifting their domicile back to India. Take, for instance, RazorPay—which was earlier registered in the US and is on track to shift its domicile to India by FY25. PhonePe is also an example in point. This company reverse-flipped from Singapore to India recently.

Now, some startups have started moving back home to India. The Indian market has undergone significant growth to provide various opportunities to startups. Also, many states are reducing bureaucratic hurdles to attract startups. At the same time, various issues relating to market operations, regulatory requirements and legal requirements by foreign countries are leading startups to move back to India.

For this chapter, we chose the case study of Crest because it provides valuable insights into why some startups opt to register abroad initially and the reasons behind their decision to reverse-flip to Bharat.

Why a $4.88M SaaS Startup Chose the US First—Then Flipped Back to India?

While planning for this chapter, we came across Crest, a SaaS startup helping D2Cs and SMBs (Small and Medium-Sized Businesses) accelerate revenue growth by enabling them to eliminate overstocking and understocking.

Like many other Indian founders who register their startups in the US, Crest's founders did the same but later registered the company back in India.

But before we delve into their entire journey of registering in the US and then flipping back, let us delve deeper into the story of Crest and how it started in the first place. Rahul Vishwakarma, the co-founder of Crest, is not a first-time entrepreneur. In fact, he started his entrepreneurial journey back in college, where he used to support the AI ecosystem by consulting with multiple companies from time to time and helping them integrate AI (artificial intelligence) and ML (machine learning) into their products. Rahul, being a chemical engineer, was a problem-solver at heart. During the Covid-19 pandemic, while running his previous startup, he noticed that there were many products that remained out of stock for days on end. People were confined to their homes and could not visit supermarkets every now and then. As a result, they started hoarding things whenever they visited these markets, maybe once every few weeks or even months. But still, these people had to compromise a lot as the products or brands they loved and wanted to purchase were unavailable in stores or online. This meant a lost opportunity for businesses and a point of frustration for consumers. While we were interviewing Rahul, he said, 'It was like we were in the early 1990s when there were no supermarkets and the neighbourhood Kirana stores only had limited inventory and few brands.' While this was a very eye-popping problem statement in Rahul's words, no one had tried to solve it.

Why Did Rahul and the Team at Crest Start with the US?

Founders and investors are always attuned to chasing big markets. It is a dream for most founders to hit the bull's-eye. Jeff Keller writes about creating your own mental movie in his bestselling book, *Attitude is Everything*.[8] An entrepreneur at heart will usually create a movie that highlights big dreams. And Rahul was an entrepreneur at heart.

So, he along with his team decided to start in the US and position themselves as a global company, whilst also building in India alongside.

Their mantra was simple: kickstart in the US and evolve into a global entity while keeping Bharat at the core.

While this was happening, they noticed two things peculiar about companies in the US. Firstly, there was always some software being used to manage their inventory. Secondly, most SMEs (small and medium enterprises) under USD 50 million in annual revenue had only one or two channels of sales. On the other hand, in India, an SME at a similar scale was already an omnichannel (selling at across more than fifteen or twenty places).

As the team at Crest moved forward, they figured out something important—being close to customers was really, really important. In the choice between going global or staying local, they decided that being near their customers was key. So, they came back to India, changing their plan to focus more on understanding and helping the people here.

Delving deeper into the insights they had garnered as mentioned above, the team at Crest realized that what they were building would have more appreciation in a country like India. Even the sales cycles were shorter, so they were selling much faster. Also, as it was a company catering to the Indian market, shifting their base back would mean easier access to capital for the unique problem they were solving.

Further, the vision they had for the business down the line matched particularly well with Indian ingredients—the parameters we spoke about earlier in this chapter.

How Should You Choose between Registering in India Versus Abroad?

Rahul quotes, 'The nature of the industry can significantly influence the decision to establish a business presence in the US versus India.' For software and enterprise companies, the US often emerges as a strategic choice due to its mature tech ecosystem, access to venture capital and a large market that is hungry for innovative solutions. A prime example is Zoho Corporation, which has successfully expanded its footprint in the software sector in the US, showcasing the potential for tech companies to thrive in that environment. Additionally, the journeys of Indian tech CEOs like Sundar Pichai, Satya Nadella and Arvind Krishna have set an example for the software industry of the success achievable in the US tech landscape.

On the other hand, industries such as fintech and consumer goods may find a robust and expansive market within India. Fintech has witnessed remarkable growth fueled by the government's digital initiatives and a population eager to embrace technological advancements in financial services. Startups like Paytm and RazorPay exemplify the success achievable in the domestic fintech space. Similarly, the consumer goods sector benefits from the vast and diverse consumer market in India, making it an attractive arena for companies to establish their roots.

Hence, entrepreneurs should maintain a balanced view, and understand the unique advantages and challenges that come with every location. It's not only just about where you start but is also about how well you understand your market and adapt to its dynamics.

Timing is also crucial. First registering abroad and entering India later in your journey can also be a strategic move. It will allow you to gauge market trends, understand global dynamics better, tailor your offerings to local needs and to capitalize on India's expansive growth potential.

While the location is a factor, it's only one part of the equation. The reverse flip worked well for Rahul as he positioned Crest as an Indian software company for homegrown clients like RR Kabel, Happilo, Plix, Furlenco and many others. It even helped to work deeper with a customer like Samosa Party, who fulfilled 95 per cent of customer demand through Crest.

Focus on solving real problems, understanding your customers and building a resilient business model will drive your startup's success, regardless of where it's located.

To sum up the chapter, we can say that the location of your startup can significantly impact its trajectory. But does it mean you should lose sleep over it? Perhaps not. The location is a piece of the puzzle, not the entire puzzle itself.

Key Takeaways

- **Location Matters but Isn't Everything:** Choosing where to register your startup can significantly impact your business. However, don't get overly fixated on location. It's one part of the equation and ultimately, the success of your startup depends on solving real problems and building a resilient model.
- **Timing the Entry Point:** Understanding when to enter a particular market can make all the difference. Sometimes, starting abroad and then moving back to India (like Crest) can be a strategic move. Timing is key.
- **Decide Carefully:** The decision on where to register your startup depends on several factors, like the legal environment, access to funding, proximity to customers and talent. Some locations provide more incentives for startups that register locally, so choose wisely based on your long-term goals.

So, What Should You Do Next?

List five factors that make your current location an advantageous or a disadvantageous place for starting up.

Also, like in the previous chapter, given below is the framework called RISING, which will guide you through Crest's journey in a nutshell:

Roadblock	**Ideal Customer**	**Solution**	**Innovation**	**Nakad (Money)**	**Growth**
Established competition and longer sales cycles for new entrants Proximity to customers was difficult to achieve from the US	SMEs, D2C brands	Inventory management system	AI-powered inventory planning and demand forecasting tool for e-commerce businesses to avoid out-of-stock, fulfill demand and grow revenue	Subscription-based model for workflows, building dashboards and integrating Crest's technology tool	Shifting back to India Increasing number of D2C brands

8

Know Your Customer (KYC)

The Thrilling Narrative of Chai Sutta Bar

In 2016, driven by passion, Anubhav Dubey and Anand Nayak founded Chai Sutta Bar (CSB),[1] a rapidly growing tea chain. Their vision was simple yet powerful—to serve India's beloved beverage, chai, in an environment-friendly manner using kulhads. Later joined by Rahul Patidar, the trio aimed to spread their unique cultural blend and values across the globe. Today, with more than 600 franchise outlets, a presence in over 370 cities and a commitment to quality and service, CSB has become a symbol of people's love and affection.

Our nation of 1.45 billion (145 crore)[2] people is divided by many cultures and traditions, but one thing binds us all: the love of chai or tea. This 'kulhad' or cup of chai transcends all socio-economic boundaries and finds its way into the hearts of millions of people. The rich, poor, middle-income folks—everyone loves it. It is more like a national beverage.

But what is it about chai that makes it more than just a beverage? What makes one so addicted to this seemingly simple drink? To answer that, we delved into the world of chai, seeking insights from an entrepreneur who could be considered a 'chai baron', a master of this beloved beverage.

As we delve into this world of chai, we will adopt the lens of 'KYC' or 'Know Your Customer', a concept that is not just a buzzword but a crucial strategy for businesses across domains. This approach will help us understand why people love chai so much and also what you should know about your customers as entrepreneurs, which will help you significantly scale your business.

Now, the natural question that might come to your mind is: how does one know their customer in and out?

Let's unravel the process. After all, *what else are we here for?*

Imagine it's past midnight and you're having one of those heart-to-heart conversations with a close friend. You know, the ones where you spill your thoughts, share your favourite memories and discuss everything under the moon. Now, think about it—you're not just talking about surface-level stuff. You're delving into the little details. What shows and movies do they love? What boy or girl do they love?

In the same way, understanding your customer is like having a late-night chat with that friend. Like you'd ask your friend about their lifestyle and what they are doing at the moment, businesses need to know their customers, their habits, their daily routines and if needed even about their dreams. Are they the quick 'on-the-go' type who need a speedy chai fix, or do they like taking their time and savouring each sip?

Knowing your customer is more than a checklist.

If you have seen the YouTube channel The BarberShop with Shantanu,[3] you must have noticed Shantanu

Deshpande, the CEO of Bombay Shaving Company,[4] trying to sell razors on the street and asking customers a lot of questions. Whatever feedback he gathers through these conversations, the team at Bombay Shaving Company makes an effort to incorporate into the product. This is a great example of being truly hands-on and listening to your customers. However, that doesn't mean they incorporate every piece of feedback. In this case, data and gut feeling also come into play.

Businesses or business owners need to actively engage with their customers and understand them in detail.

But Why Is 'Knowing Your Customer' Important Afterall?

Even if you have an excellent product, people will only buy it if they want or need it. You've got to understand what your customers truly want. Customers need a reason to pick you over others. It could be super-fast delivery, discounts or having exactly what satisfies customers' needs and desires. It's about becoming a part of their lives, and providing solutions that truly matter to them.

Remember: It's not about what you sell. It's about why they buy.

Before we dive deeper into the chapter and introduce you to the protagonist (the entrepreneurs), here's a list of five things you absolutely need to know about your customers. These are essential questions you should ask yourself before moving forward in your journey to truly understanding your customers.

1. **Who Are They?**
   It's crucial to understand who your customers really are. Take *Licious*, for instance—they target urban, health-conscious individuals who are looking for fresh, high-quality meat delivered right to their doorsteps. If you know your audience's age, location and lifestyle, you can create marketing that really clicks with them. It's all about making sure your message speaks directly to them, whether they're young professionals in cities or families in smaller towns.
2. **What Do They Do?**
   Knowing what your customers do—their jobs, hobbies and everyday habits—helps shape your product or service. For example, *Saffola* (a popular brand in the edible oil segment) knows that many Indians are becoming more health-conscious. That's why their oils are marketed as a healthy alternative for busy professionals and homemakers who still want tasty, nutritious meals. When you understand your customers' interests, you can tailor your marketing to show them how your product fits into their daily routines.
3. **Why Do They Buy?**
   Understanding why your customers make a purchase is key to speaking their language. Think about *Zomato*—they know that people aren't just ordering food because they're hungry but because they want a quick, easy and reliable way to satisfy cravings, enjoy variety or celebrate a special occasion. By understanding the reasons behind a purchase,

you can highlight exactly what your product or service does for them—whether it's convenience, quality or even emotional satisfaction.

4. **When Do They Buy?**
   Timing can be everything. Take *Zepto*, for example. They have tapped into the ultra-fast delivery market, catering to customers who need products delivered in under ten minutes. With many of their customers living in metro cities, *Zepto* understands that people don't have time to wait for hours or spend effort finding what they need urgently. By recognizing when and why their customers need fast deliveries, *Zepto* has tailored its entire business model to meet this urgent demand, ensuring that its service is relevant whenever the need arises and whatever it might be!
5. **How Do They Buy?**
   The way your customers prefer to shop matters more than you might think. Take HealthifyMe as an example. They've built a comprehensive health and fitness platform, offering services like online fitness coaching, personalized nutrition plans and health tracking. Many of their customers prefer to make purchases directly through the app, whether it's for fitness sessions, diet plans or tracking their health goals. By focusing on an easy-to-navigate mobile platform, HealthifyMe makes it simple for customers to access their services anytime, anywhere, enhancing convenience and customer satisfaction.

Now that we have explored these five essential questions, the time has finally come to introduce you to the protagonist. Meet Anubhav Dubey.

The Journey of Anubhav and Chai Sutta Bar: Serving Chai, One Kulhad at a Time

If you are still in college, you might have friends preparing for competitive exams such as the UPSC or MBA entrance exams, such as CAT and XAT. Some might also be thinking of starting their own businesses or ventures.

While in college, many people are enthusiastic, with age on their side and a zeal to make a mark. Young people don't just study but also dream of making a difference in the world. After classes, a different kind of adventure begins. Some students, armed with ambition and business ideas, are not just thinking about getting a job. They see their age as an advantage, a time to take risks and leave their mark. The energy to create something new drives them to explore ideas no one has tried before.

This was the story of Anubhav Dubey, a young soul born in the heartland of Madhya Pradesh, Rewa district, in 1993. However, Anubhav's journey was destined to deviate from the conventional paths etched by his family. Despite a business-oriented lineage, his father's vision painted a different future, one in which Anubhav would become an esteemed IAS officer.

Fuelled by familial expectations, Anubhav found himself in the bustling streets of Delhi, fervently preparing for the UPSC exams. But, as fate would have it, the corridors of bureaucracy weren't to be his only route. Faced with the challenges of competitive exams, Anubhav stood at a crossroads, his dreams of a nine-to-five job fading against the allure of entrepreneurship.

Anubhav had big dreams to start something of his own, but was stuck between his family's expectations and his own dreams. So, along with his friend Anand, he decided to take a leap of faith. They chose to pursue their dreams. For this, they chose to pursue their dream and start a business. They brainstormed various ideas and settled on something universally loved—tea! With just a modest sum they had saved up, they opened a humble tea stall in Indore in 2016.

When you wake up, you need tea (chai). When you come home exhausted from work, you're in desperate need of tea. From the fanciest restaurants to the littlest dhabas, chai is everywhere.

Anubhav and Anand, armed with a small investment of Rs 3 lakh, embarked on their tea business. They were well aware of their financial limitations, understanding that they couldn't afford any marketing, interior design or branding. But this didn't deter them. They decided to proceed with their idea and opened a small outlet outside a girls' hostel in Indore. They borrowed items from others and used a simple wooden plank with 'Chai Sutta Bar' handwritten on it. To their delight, this humble setup worked like a charm, proving that success can be achieved even with limited resources. This cafe with a handwritten board started getting so famous for its unique name that sometimes, they couldn't handle the rush.

Now, Why Should Your Customers Need You and Only You?

Every business strives to answer a crucial question: why should customers choose them over competitors? The answer lies in a Unique Sales Proposition (USP). Your USP is the distinctive element that makes your business stand out in the market, giving customers a compelling reason to choose you. Identifying your USP involves completing the phrase, 'Customers will buy from me because my business is the only __________.' (fill in the blank)

Your USP can evolve with changes in your business or the market, and you may have different USPs for different customer segments. These USPs can be effective because they are driven by what the customer looks for when buying. It's a good idea to review your USPs regularly.

Can you tailor your products or services to match your customers' needs better? Consider asking your customers why they buy from you. This will tell you what they think your USP is—this may differ from what you think your USP is.

It's also useful to constantly check what your competitor is doing. Remember—if your competitors are doing the same things as you, your USP is no longer your USP. At this point, you either need to strengthen your USP or your core or build another moat that can augment your existing USP.

The best way to KYC is through talking to your customers, being with them and spending time with them. Because when you are building a company, you need to have that sort of discipline to know the real problems and pain points of your customers. After all, they are the ones you are building the company for.

The Viral Hacks Behind the CSB Virality

If you want to impress your customers, you need to know them. As simple as that.

Anubhav and Anand understood this well, which is why Chai Sutta Bar was able to capture the attention of its customers and become incredibly popular.

But the question is: how did they truly understand their customers and turn that understanding into virality?

Well for that, they started deploying the following marketing strategy:

1. **Word of Mouth and Social Proof:** Anubhav and Anand demonstrated their entrepreneurial ingenuity by inviting friends and playing music to create a bustling atmosphere, sparking curiosity among passers-by. This clever tactic led people to believe there was something unique about the place, contributing to its initial success.
2. **Free Tea:** On the first day, they offered free tea, which was an irresistible draw. Once people experienced the quality, they were more likely to return as paying customers.
3. **Organic Growth:** Their marketing relied heavily on word of mouth and the organic buzz created by the initial free offerings and strategic location of their outlets, mainly right in front of girls' hostels at various locations.
4. **Name and Branding:** 'Chai Sutta Bar' cleverly played on words. While 'sutta' is Hindi slang for a cigarette, in Chai Sutta Bar's context, it denoted principles or basics, creating a unique and memorable brand identity.

Despite the word 'sutta' in their name, they did not sell cigarettes, maintaining a focus on tea and related products.

After Chai Sutta Bar started gaining immense popularity, the next step was to expand the business and open outlets in other cities across Bharat. However, in a country where chai preferences change every 100 kilometres, the challenge lies in making standardization scalable while respecting regional tastes.

Recognizing the importance of local flavours, they embarked on a comprehensive market research journey, uncovering each new city's unique tastes and consumption patterns. They thought of keeping some chai varieties common across geographies and introducing special chai catering to local tastes, thereby fostering a sense of connection with local communities.

In the food and beverage space, especially in quick service restaurant (QSR) chains, standardization is not just a preference, it's a necessity. Anubhav and Anand had to be committed to ensuring that every cup of chai served met the same high standards and same taste, regardless of location, so that they could instil confidence in the quality of their product. This was needed to ensure that they could scale.

To achieve this standardization, Anubhav and Anand knew they had to go beyond just recipes. They focused on standardization through stories and detailed Standard Operating Procedures (SOPs). By crafting these narratives around their core chai varieties, they ensured that each cup told the same story, creating a uniform customer experience.

With their deep-rooted research into understanding the product and customer, 'Chai Sutta Bar' has achieved remarkable success. Today, it boasts 600 stores across the world and serves over 4.5 lakh 'kulhad chai' every day.[5]

Anubhav and Anand spotted an opportunity to make chai trendy among Bharat's youth. By focusing on what young people in urban areas value—authentic yet modern experiences—they aimed to make chai cool and appealing. This strategic move laid the foundation for broader customer interest as their business expanded, an authentication of the power of understanding your initial customers.

Now, Chai Sutta Bar is that one startup that aptly utilized the concepts of KYC, USP, customer needs and market requirements fully to their advantage. Your attention is again drawn to the fact that despite using the word 'sutta', they managed to keep their clientele away from provision of the same and yet made their venture a success. The word 'sutta' may have drawn many a customer to their outlets, but they succeeded in satisfying their craving with a preferred choice of tea instead.

And no one's complaining. Get your own sutta, if you want to. But the question is, should you?

Key Takeaways

- **Time It Right:** Recognize when your customers are most likely to buy and plan accordingly.
- **Know Your Audience:** Misidentifying your audience can lead to wasted resources, ineffective marketing and brand damage.
- **Communicate with Customers:** Have real conversations with customers to uncover insights beyond mere assumptions. Start selling razors on the street like Shantanu did.
- **Leverage Your Social Circle:** Involve your friends to create a buzz and attract customers just like Anubhav and Anand did.

So, What Should You Do Next?

Identify your customers using the 5Ws framework: Who they are, what they need, when they face challenges, where they seek help and why they would choose you. Note down the answers to these questions in the rough space given below.

Also, like in the previous chapter, given below is the framework called RISING, which will guide you through Chai Sutta Bar's journey in a nutshell:

Roadblock	Ideal Customer	Solution	Innovation	Nakad (Money)	Growth
Financial constraints Negative brand perception at the beginning Raids by authorities	Young people, particularly college students and young professional, living in urban areas	Unique branding, variety in flavours of tea	Varied tea flavours	Selling chai and related products, focusing on high-volume sales through multiple outlets	Expanded the platform to different regions, leveraging smart techniques such as YouTube content creation 600 stores in 370 cities worldwide within eight years

9

Acquiring Your First 100 Customers

The Journey of the Unicorn, BharatPe

BharatPe[1] is more than just a fintech company—it is a revolutionary force transforming the way India does business. By providing digital payment and financial services to small merchants and grocery stores, BharatPe has empowered millions of businesses to embrace the digital economy. Starting as a simple QR code-based payments solution, BharatPe has grown into a financial powerhouse, offering merchant loans, card payment acceptance and a suite of innovative financial products. Its mission? To uplift the unorganized retail sector in India and propel it into the digital age. Today, BharatPe has earned the coveted 'unicorn' status, symbolizing its monumental success and its unparalleled contributions to India's entrepreneurial ecosystem.

The story of BharatPe began in 2018, a time when India was witnessing the early waves of a digital payments revolution fuelled by the launch of the mobile wallet-based payments. Amid this transformation, BharatPe dared to dream big. It became one of India's first companies to introduce India's first UPI interoperable QR code and the first zero MDR payment acceptance service.

This single all-in-one QR code allowed merchants to accept payments from any payment app, breaking barriers and setting a new standard for payment systems in the country.

The engine behind this revolution is UPI, a marvel of modern technology. UPI has become so engrained in our daily lives that we barely notice its impact any more. Whether it's a chai stall on the corner, a vegetable vendor in a bustling market or a high-end retail store, BharatPe's QR codes have become ubiquitous.

Imagine a chaiwallah proudly displaying a BharatPe QR code, knowing he can accept payments from any app without hassle. Or a *kirana* store owner who can now access affordable loans facilitated through BharatPe.

What sets BharatPe apart is its deep understanding of the needs of Bharat. By focusing on simplicity, accessibility and trust, BharatPe has built a platform that merchants not only use but rely on.

As UPI gained traction in India, a critical gap in the digital payment ecosystem was becoming evident. While platforms such as Paytm, PhonePe and Google Pay focused on consumers, no one was addressing the unique needs of merchants. These business owners, who form the backbone of India's economy, were left without adequate solutions that could cater to their challenges. Moreover, the lack of interoperability between QR codes issued by different payment platforms added to the inefficiencies.

BharatPe identified this opportunity and stepped in with a groundbreaking solution—a single interoperable

QR code. This innovation enabled merchants to accept payments from any digital payments app. For the first time, small business owners could offer digital payment options without worrying about compatibility or app-specific constraints. This simplified the payments system and bridged a critical gap, making digital transactions accessible and practical for merchants.

But BharatPe didn't stop there. Understanding the financial needs of small businesses, it expanded its services to include facilitating merchant loans, card payment acceptance and other financial products. This holistic approach empowered merchants to grow their businesses while seamlessly integrating them into the digital economy.

The Merchant and the Magic of Simplicity

A customer is someone who purchases an item of their choice, while a merchant is the individual or business selling that item. Merchants range from small street vendors to large retailers and form the backbone of commerce.

To illustrate the challenges merchants face, let's take a historical detour to the seventeenth-century Dutch Golden Age and the infamous tulip mania.[2]

During this period, tulip bulbs were traded at sky-high prices due to a speculative frenzy. These speculative bubbles happen when people get caught up in excitement and invest in something without fully understanding its value. During this time, the price of tulip bulbs rose to extreme levels as people believed they were incredibly valuable. Some even traded their land or life savings for a single bulb. But in February 1637, the market crashed, leaving many people in financial trouble.

Just as the tulip market needed stability, the digital payment industry needed a simple, standardized system to make things easier for users and encourage more people to use it. Without such solutions, both systems faced challenges and inefficiencies.

Now, imagine a modern parallel—India's early digital payment landscape. With the advent of digital payments via mobile wallets, platforms such as Paytm, PhonePe and Google Pay created a wave of enthusiasm. But this excitement soon revealed a fragmented ecosystem: each app came with its own QR code, forcing users to download multiple apps to make payments. This made it inconvenient for users and slowed adoption.

The lack of interoperability mirrored the inefficiencies of the tulip mania—excitement without structure, potential without accessibility. This friction hindered widespread adoption, especially among merchants who sought simplicity and reliability in payment systems.

It was amidst this chaos that BharatPe emerged as a game-changer. With a single, interoperable QR code that worked across all payment apps, BharatPe eliminated complexity for merchants and customers alike. This simple yet powerful innovation transformed the digital payment landscape, enabling merchants to adopt cashless transactions effortlessly.

How Did BharatPe's Remarkable Journey Begin?

Changing age-old practices is never easy, especially for merchants accustomed to traditional methods of business. Yet, Shashvat Nakrani, the visionary behind BharatPe, achieved just that.

Being born in a Gujarati family, Shashvat, was exposed to business conversations since childhood. Naturally, he developed a passion and interest in business, which further became his ambition.

He says, 'In our part of the country, business is a very respected profession and people have great regard for it.' As they would like to say it in Gujarati, '*Karna hai toh dhandho karna hai* (If we have to do something, we will do a business).'

Shashvat's curiosity and thirst for knowledge fetched him a seat in one of the most-coveted IITs. He started pursuing his bachelor's in textile technology from IIT Delhi. While his weekdays were mostly jam-packed with classes, seminars and lab sessions, he had time to go out with his friends on the weekends to break the monotony.

While the purpose of going out was to have fun, that business mentality always led Shashvat to observe the unobserved. UPI was in its infancy at that time, yet Shashvat saw its transformative potential. He noticed how merchants struggled with digital payments, navigating the fragmented ecosystem of multiple apps and QR codes. This observation planted the seed for BharatPe.

Shashvat wasn't just looking to create a product; he wanted to solve a pressing problem. His vision was clear: build a unified, merchant-first platform that simplifies payments and empowers small businesses.

Riding the Wave of Innovation

The journey had officially begun, and Shashvat was ready to chart a new course with BharatPe. Around the same time, Tez (now Google Pay) had just gone viral.

Tez utilized a technology called audio QR (AQR) to facilitate device pairing for money transfers. This innovative method involved the app generating, encrypting and sending random audio bursts through a device's speaker, which were then captured and decoded by the recipient device's microphone for seamless pairing. Later rebranded as Google Pay after its acquisition by Google, Tez gained massive popularity, driven by its generous cashback rewards that attracted millions of users to download the app.

For Shashvat, the signs were clear: the Indian government was determined to push digital payments forward. This was an unmissable opportunity.

'If the government is so invested in this ecosystem, I need to build something around it,' Shashvat thought. With this insight, he and his friends began visiting markets across Delhi, searching for real-world problems to solve.

They quickly realized a key truth: competing with established giants like Google Pay or PhonePe, armed with their billion-dollar cashback budgets, was impractical. Instead, they needed to think differently.

A Eureka Moment

During their visits to bustling Delhi markets, they made a startling observation. While digital payments were gaining traction among consumers for peer-to-peer payments, merchants were hardly using it. The benefits of digital payments simply weren't being marketed to them effectively.

This was the lightbulb moment. Merchants weren't the problem—there was an untapped opportunity to empower them by simplifying digital payments.

Shashvat and his friends returned to IIT Delhi, energized by this insight. Determined to test their idea, they began visiting campus shops and nearby markets with a simple prototype.

Their approach was ingenious yet straightforward. They downloaded the BHIM app on shopkeepers' phones, printed QR codes for their accounts and pasted them on shopfronts. To make the process even more appealing, they added the logos of popular payment apps like PhonePe and Paytm alongside the message: 'All payment apps accepted here.'

With this, they had their prototype ready. The next step? Testing it in the real world.

Proving the Concept

Excited yet nervous, Shashvat and his friends stood outside the shops where they had pasted the QR codes. They observed transactions closely, nudging customers to use the QR codes instead of cash, explaining the benefits of speed and convenience.

To their amazement, it worked. Customers began scanning the codes, and merchants started receiving payments. The biggest surprise for the merchants? 'How are people able to pay using any app through the same QR code?'

The merchants were thrilled. And for Shashvat and his team, this validation was electrifying. They had created something simple yet revolutionary—a solution that could transform the way merchants accepted payments.

That night, Shashvat and his friends likely had the most satisfying sleep of their lives—or perhaps no sleep at all, as they were buzzing with excitement.

What began as an experiment soon turned into a mission. For two weeks, Shashvat and his friends tirelessly repeated this process—visiting shops, refining their prototype and proving its potential. By the end of this period, they were convinced that they were on the cusp of building something truly monumental.

Following this, Shashvat and his team started hiring people who would go out on the street and to each shop and onboard merchants. They adopted a market-by-market onboarding approach, similar to the strategies used in the FMCG (fast-moving consumer goods) industry. This method was target-based and the salesforce received incentives for meeting their targets.

Soon, this led them to achieve their first 100 merchants onboarded.

Understanding the reluctance of merchants towards going digital, they simplified their offering to a static printed QR code with a stand—the design now commonly seen in shops across India. This innovation resonated deeply with merchants, as it required minimal effort and seamlessly enabled instant payment settlements directly into their bank accounts.

This simplicity, combined with the trust merchants gained from receiving payments instantly, laid the foundation for BharatPe's value proposition.

Building the First Scalable Product

The team began coding and launched an initial version of the product. However, their planned user flow didn't resonate with merchants. This revealed a crucial insight into their target audience:

Merchants don't take the initiative to adopt digital systems on their own. They're accustomed to their existing methods and need solutions served directly to them.

Initially, BharatPe introduced a digital QR code on their merchant app but soon realized it was cumbersome for merchants to use. In response, they innovated and launched physical QR codes that could be placed on counters or walls. Simplifying further, they developed the now-common static printed QR code with a stand, making it easy for merchants to display. This simple yet effective design resonated strongly, as it required minimal effort and enabled instant payment settlements directly into merchants' bank accounts.

This simplicity, combined with the trust merchants gained from receiving payments instantly, laid the foundation for BharatPe's value proposition.

However, onboarding merchants came with its own set of challenges. Most shop owners were passive and reluctant to engage with new processes. To overcome this, BharatPe adopted an aggressive and hands-on approach:

1. **On-Ground Salesforce**
   Shashvat and his team hired a dedicated salesforce to visit shops and onboard merchants directly. These sales reps demonstrated the benefits of BharatPe's system and personally assisted merchants in getting started.
2. **Market-by-Market Strategy**
   Borrowing tactics from the FMCG sector, the team focused on specific markets, targeting one area at

a time. This localized approach allowed them to build momentum and gain visibility in key regions.

3. **Incentive-Driven Targets**
   The salesforce operated on a target-based model, with incentives for hitting their goals, ensuring high motivation and performance.
4. **Customer Support**
   BharatPe launched a 24/7 customer care line to address any issues merchants faced. While initial volumes were low due to the slow adoption of digital payments at the time, this proactive support created trust among early users.

Key Lessons from BharatPe's Early Days

1. **Understand Your Customers**
   Merchants in India were hesitant to adopt new technologies, so BharatPe tailored its solution to their specific needs, prioritizing simplicity and ease of use.
2. **Focus on Immediate Value**
   By offering instant payment settlements and a straightforward interface, BharatPe demonstrated clear and tangible benefits to merchants right from the start.
3. **Adopt a Hands-on Approach**
   Direct engagement with merchants allowed the team to build trust, gather feedback and iterate quickly on their product.
4. **Be Ready to Pivot**
   The initial product didn't work as planned, but BharatPe's ability to adapt led to the introduction of the static QR code, a game-changing innovation.

5. **Solve for Scale**
   BharatPe's decision to hire an on-ground salesforce and adopt a market-specific strategy enabled them to scale rapidly and reach merchants nationwide.
6. **Leverage Data for Growth**
   The introduction of merchant lending based on transaction insights not only addressed a major gap but also created new revenue streams.

Takeaways for Aspiring Entrepreneurs

- Focus on **neglected customer segments** to solve problems that others overlook.
- Ensure your product is **simple and easy to adopt,** especially for less tech-savvy users.
- Be agile and willing to pivot based on user feedback.
- Showcase **immediate benefits** to win over early adopters.
- Build trust by addressing customers' pain points and evolving with their needs.

Take inspiration from BharatPe's journey and start mapping out how you'll acquire your first 100 customers. Use the RISING Framework to guide your strategy:

1. **Roadblock:** Identify the primary barriers your target audience faces.
2. **Ideal Customer:** Define your target audience clearly.
3. **Solution:** Offer a straightforward and impactful solution.
4. **Innovation:** Differentiate your product with unique features or benefits.

5. **Nakad (Money):** Design a sustainable revenue model.
6. **Growth:** Develop a scalable plan to expand your reach and impact.

BharatPe's story is a testament to the power of perseverance, adaptability and a deep understanding of your customers. Let it inspire you to build your own revolutionary idea—one step at a time.

Remember: The journey might be tough, but when the going gets tough, the tough get going.

10

Pricing, the Holy Grail of Business

How Does Boult Sell Products Every Three Seconds?

Boult[1] *is one of India's fastest-growing wearable brands. It is a young company conceived in June 2017 to make a difference in the way consumers experience sound in their everyday lives. This passion for creating exceptional experiences has led them to become one of the top three audio brands in India, selling a product every three seconds.*

Have you ever wanted to buy your favourite thing but couldn't because of the price?

We all want to buy many things in our life at various stages but may not be able to afford them due to their price. And often, we realize that the particular item or product, though affordable at the price displayed, is actually not worth the amount. So, this pricing of an item becomes an overriding consideration in the decision to buy that product or not, besides its requirement.

The Business of Pricing

A lot of people dream of starting their own business with the aim of earning a lot of money. This earning is based on the profits earned in the business, which, in turn, depends on the demand for the item, the quality provided, and most importantly the 'right pricing'.

In this chapter we will be focusing on the aspect of pricing and how it impacts sales and business. Why is the pricing of a product or service one of the most important considerations of a business?

To answer that, we need to understand the fundamental theory of demand and supply. You have a product or a service to sell and you have customers in need of that product or service. In other words, there is demand and supply at play here.

But in order for the supply to be consumed by the demand profitably, one needs to set the right price, besides the other aspects. If the pricing is not correct, you won't have the product or service selling as envisaged. Moreover, pricing has a lot of implications regarding how your probable customers view your product or service.

Set the price too high—people might see the product or service as not worth it.

Set the price too low—customers might doubt the quality and think that it has been priced 'cheap' because of low quality.

Price affects customer perception of the item and perception is dynamic. Setting the right perception while starting a new business or diversifying your existing businesses' product line is paramount.

If you have seen the movie *Jerry Maguire*, you would have noticed Tom Cruise and Cuba Gooding Jr yelling 'Show me the money!' at each other over the phone.

Similar is the case with the consumer. They want to know the price of a product before making a decision to purchase.

Whenever we go to buy a product as customers, we may encounter the following decision-making questions:

- Would we purchase these products had they been priced slightly higher or lower?
- Would we switch to an alternative shop, store or brand altogether if we found a cheaper alternative?
- Would we prefer a discount on these products?
- What else could impact our decision to purchase or not purchase a particular item?
- What is our switching cost in terms of use case/benefit that we could derive from the products, but couldn't because of moving to another brand for the same item?

To answer these very pertinent questions, we approached the founders of a startup, whose business is thriving in a highly fragmented market. We thought it would be a good idea to speak to one of the leading players in the wearables and audio segment about the various aspects of pricing and the process of trying different pricing models and strategies.

The answers and knowledge of the subject is straight from the horse's mouth as given in the succeeding paragraphs. We got to learn about the fragmented audio and wearables market, and how creating a brand and setting the right price for a product could be the turning point for a business through the journey of Varun and Tarun Gupta, the co-founders of Boult.

But, before we dive into the story of these founders, let us take a look at the audio and wearables market in India and what makes it a truly fragmented space to begin with. India's rising internet use led to a boom in this industry. The Covid-19 pandemic also contributed to this boom as it resulted in lockdowns, where people had to stay indoors. The use of wireless audio equipment for entertainment increased. Also, the rise in video streaming and remote working, remote learning and home workouts increased the need for wireless audio equipment.

These factors led to multiple new brands, both local and global, emerging in the audio and wearables space in India.

How Did Boult Bootstrap Its Way to ₹750 Crore in Revenue and Become One of the Leading Players?

Venturing into the e-commerce space by offering consulting services to startups and brands, Boult co-founders and brothers Varun and Tarun Gupta realized the massive potential of e-commerce and online shopping as a whole.

While working with numerous brands, Varun got educated with the following plus points of any e-commerce business:

1. Massive Cost Arbitrage
2. Wide Reach

3. Global Market Access
4. Data-Driven Decision-Making
5. Personalization and Recommendations

Varun soon realized that there was an opportunity, a market big enough to create something special in the audio wearables industry that would grow into a burgeoning business and brand.

An audio buff, who used to play the guitar, Varun—with three previous startups already under his belt, teamed up with Tarun to venture into the audio wear space with Boult, a successful startup today.

However, things were not as easy when he started, since there were too many players and brands out there offering similar products at different price points. The co-founders just didn't know where to start. There were too many data points—enough to confuse even a seasoned entrepreneur. And, both Varun and Tarun were just starting out.

But after doing some thorough primary and secondary research, they realized that although there were too many players offering the same products in the TWS (True Wireless Stereo) market, none were that combined premium looks and superior sound quality at a price point comparable to other brands.

The market was dominated by globally reputed brands, including Sennheiser, AKG, Bose, Harman Kardon and Marshall, along with some local manufacturers. Yet there was a noticeable gap, which Varun and Tarun could fill.

But they got stuck on one question: '*Theek hai yaar, hum achha product bana toh lenge, par usko kis daam par bechen?*

Market mein toh har tarah ki pricing ke earphones already available hain [We will be able to build a great product, but at what price would we sell it? After all, there are many products across all price ranges in the market].' Such dilemmas are faced by many entrepreneurs, especially in a country like ours, where the markets are highly fragmented. This means that there are many products in the same category across various price points.

Now, with India being a highly price sensitive market, where most consumers consider price as the major factor before making any purchase decision, striking a balance between quality and price becomes really tough and tricky. So, how did Boult do it?

Boult's Balancing Act: Balancing Quality and Price

Boult started looking at some other models for pricing. It examined both the cost-plus pricing model, where you first calculate the total cost to make a product and then add a profit margin to set the selling price and the target costing model, where you start by deciding on the selling price based on market conditions and then work backwards to ensure the manufacturing cost is low enough to make a profit at that price.

A great example to understand this is to look at the picture above which shows how costs are added alongside margins to arrive at final price.

Besides this, Boult preferred the target-costing model, which involves determining the price customers would be willing to pay and then keeping manufacturing costs low to ensure profitability.

Business Revenue	Price (₹)	% of Total Orders	Cost to Produce (₹), 60%	Margin (₹), 40%
Product 1	500	20%	300	200
Product 2	1000	20%	600	400
Product 3	2000	20%	1200	800
Product 4	5000	20%	3000	2000
Product 5	10000	20%	6000	4000
Revenue per sale, avg	3500	-	-	-
Cost to produce, avg	-	-	2200	-

Metric	Jan-25	Feb-25	Mar-25	Apr-25	May-25	Jun-25
Number of Sales	100	130	170	210	260	310
Sales growth MoM, %	-	30%	31%	24%	24%	19%
Revenue (₹)	350000	455000	595000	735000	910000	1085000
Total Cost to Produce (₹)	210000	273000	357000	441000	546000	651000
Shipping Costs (₹)	20000	25000	30000	35000	40000	45000
Transaction Fee (3%)	10500	13650	17850	22050	27300	32550
Total Costs (₹)	240500	311650	404850	498050	613300	728550
Net Income (₹)	109500	143350	190150	236950	296700	356450
Net Margin	31%	31%	32%	32%	33%	33%
Total Revenue Cumulative	350000	805000	1400000	2135000	3045000	4130000
Total Net Income Cumulative	109500	252850	443000	679950	976650	1333100

This was a low-capex model, as one could avoid large initial investments in factories or expensive equipment by using cost-effective, flexible methods such as outsourcing production. Varun and Tarun were very particular about avoiding large capital expenditures that could negatively affect their profits and losses. During our chat with Varun, he said, 'It is crucial to stay profitable because if you're not, it can really hurt your morale and make it tough to keep the business going, especially if you don't secure funding.'

They focused on two main principles to stay successful. Firstly, they avoided falling into the trap of over-innovation and getting stuck in the loop of analysis-paralysis. Secondly, they started small and focused on generating a few lakh rupees in revenue and achieving some level of profitability. This helped them build confidence and gradually invest in making the products unique. Varun said, 'If you don't have much investment or funding, you cannot afford to start with a highly differentiated product.'These principles ensured that they were profitable from day one, focusing on design differentiation but not trying to create something entirely new. Instead, they offered similar products at a lower price, which attracted customers. They also focused and still focus on the following parameters while carrying out this balancing act.

Product Design and Innovation

- Boult focuses on designing products that offer high-quality features at affordable prices. By investing in R&D and understanding market needs, they create products that meet consumer expectations without exorbitant costs.

Cost-Effective Production

- Utilizing efficient manufacturing processes and economies of scale helps Boult keep production costs low. Sourcing components strategically and maintaining strong supplier relationships contribute to reducing costs while maintaining quality.

Direct-to-Consumer Model

- Boult employs a D2C model, minimizing intermediaries and reducing markups. This model allows them to offer competitive pricing while retaining higher control over customer experience and quality assurance.

For businesses without significant funding, setting your prices wisely is crucial. You can't spend a fortune on manufacturing costs and then decide on the price. You need money for marketing, distribution, testing and handling returns. Setting these precedents before making the product is essential. A common challenge for young entrepreneurs is the temptation to keep profits for themselves when they see good unit economics. Instead, it's better to reinvest those profits into the business to ensure growth and maintain a competitive edge.

In a competitive market like the audio industry, pricing is just one factor. The real differentiator, however, lies in premium quality and premium sound, which Boult offers. Take a look at the audio category in India. As shown in the table below, almost all the brands (names anonymized) fall within the same price range. The true differentiators here could be factors like quality, design or innovation. Even in a price-sensitive market, innovation is the key to standing out. This innovation could range from distinct design language or enhanced features that not only help differentiate your product but also set trends, build a cult following, expand your reach, attract more customers and enhance your distribution strategy.

Product Category	Brand A	Boult	Brand B	Brand C
True Wireless Earbuds	₹999 – ₹4,999	₹799 – ₹3,000	₹599 – ₹2,500	₹1,199 – ₹4,999
Over-Ear Headphones	₹1,199 – ₹6,000	₹999 – ₹3,500	₹799 – ₹2,000	₹1,499 – ₹5,999
Wired Earphones	₹299 – ₹1,500	₹349 – ₹1,500	₹299 – ₹1,000	₹499 – ₹1,499

How Should Entrepreneurs Think about Pricing a New Product?

The strategy for pricing a new product goes far beyond just numbers and requires a comprehensive understanding of the market, customer perceptions and the unique value your product offers. Entrepreneurs must consider a multitude of factors to arrive at a price that aligns with both their business objectives and market dynamics.

First and foremost, pricing should be grounded in thorough market analysis. Understanding the target segment's purchasing power, their preferences and the options already available in the market is essential. The price must be in consonance with the production costs, marketing expenses, labour, overheads and other operational expenditures to ensure the business remains profitable. A deep dive into competitors' pricing strategies can provide an insight into market expectations and can guide the entrepreneur to position their product effectively.

However, pricing is not just about staying competitive but is also about establishing the perceived value of your product. Entrepreneurs need to be confident in the unique value their product brings to the table. What problem does it solve? How does it set itself apart from similar options in the market? The answers to these questions form the core of your pricing strategy and should influence every decision along the way.

When considering pricing, there are several strategies to choose from. These range from cost-plus pricing, where a markup is added to the cost of production, to more sophisticated approaches like skimming pricing, penetration pricing and bundling. Each of these strategies comes with its own set of benefits and risks, and the choice depends largely on the startup's goals, the market conditions and the sentiments of the target audience.

For instance, if the goal is rapid customer acquisition, penetration pricing—setting a low price to attract customers quickly—may be the way to go. For example, the initial launch price of Sony's PlayStation 3 was around Rs 45,000, with its principal rival XBOX 360 selling its product at an initially lower price. However, PlayStation 3's price gradually dropped to Rs 25,000 when XBOX rivalled PS3 with their simpler approach to gaming and increased compatibility.[2]

If the objective is to position the product as a premium offering, skimming pricing—where the price starts high and decreases over time—could create the desired exclusivity. For example, Netflix slashed its basic plan by 60.12 per cent from Rs 499 monthly to Rs 199 monthly to attract masses in India.[3]

Similarly, bundling can help increase perceived value, driving higher sales volume by offering a set of products at a discounted price.

Ultimately, the pricing strategy should align with the startup's long-term vision and its understanding of the market. Entrepreneurs need to be clear about the problem their product solves, confident in its unique value and adaptive to market feedback. Pricing is an always-on and a dynamic activity that may evolve as the startup grows, but it must always reflect the true worth of the product in the eyes of the customer while ensuring the business's financial health. So, keep a feedback loop with your customers to learn about the value you add or where you can add more. This will help you determine how to evolve your pricing model over time.

Key Takeaways

- **Perception Is the Game:** How you price your product will impact how customers perceive its value. High prices may suggest premium quality, while low prices may raise doubts about quality.
- **Build Momentum:** Begin with a smaller scope, focusing on early profitability rather than trying to build the perfect product from day one. Profitability can help build momentum and confidence.
- **Balance It Out:** Striking the right balance between price and product features is essential, especially in price-sensitive markets like India. This helps build trust and attracts customers.
- **Don't Overanalyze:** Don't get bogged down with over-innovating or trying to perfect the product. Focus on delivering a good product that meets market demand and drives revenue.
- **Keep Adding Fuel:** Instead of keeping early profits, reinvest them in the business to fuel growth. This keeps the business competitive and sustainable over time.

So, What Should You Do Next?

Prepare a list of each item you bought in the ranges of 0–100, 100–1000,1000–5000, 5000 and above. List reasons why you bought it and write yes in case you would repurchase the item if the price increases. Study that 'why' and apply the same principles whenever you start.

Also, like in the previous chapter, given below is the framework called RISING, which will guide you through Boult's journey in detail:

Roadblock	Ideal Customer	Solution	Innovation	Nakad (Money)	Growth
Market saturation	Tech-savvy consumers	Quality and affordability	Design differentiation	Reinvestment of profits	Product line expansion
Pricing dilemma	Price-conscious buyers	Direct-to-consumer model		Target costing model	
Product differentiation					

11

Skyrocketing Your Distribution

The Sneakerhead Who Sells to Ranbir Kapoor and Ranveer Singh

India's premier streetwear fashion destination Mainstreet Marketplace[1] *deals in premium luxury apparel, redefining sneaker culture in the country by making exclusive kicks from Yeezy, Jordan, Anti-Social Social Club, Adidas, Nike, etc., more accessible to the niche-yet-prevalent market of sneakerheads. They have gone on to raise USD 2 million (around Rs 16 crore) in a seed funding round from investors, including Zomato CEO Deepinder Goyal, Zerodha co-founder Nikhil Kamath, Spotify India MD Amarjit Singh Batra and several other angel investors and social media influencers. With celebrity clients like Ranbir Kapoor, Karan Johar and Ranveer Singh, Mainstreet Marketplace has established itself as a trendsetter in India's evolving sneaker and streetwear scene.*

It is not easy to sneak into someone else's space, more so into their hearts. The attempt is fraught with the dangers of getting caught and prosecuted or rejected by the heart that doesn't like you.

This chapter, however, is dedicated to one such 'sneaker'—a bold entrepreneur who stormed into the business of fashion and won the hearts of millions in India. How? By tapping into a market that was conveniently oblivious to a product that would soon become a staple: sneakers.

Now, as we delved deeper into the concept of KYC in the chapter on Chai Sutta Bar, we realized that distribution is a natural extension of truly understanding your customer. But why are we talking about distribution here? Because the success of any product isn't just about knowing the customer, but is about being present where they are, when they need you most. Just as the nineteenth century was defined by the industrial revolution and the twentieth century by production, the twenty-first century is all about distribution.

Earlier distribution models were just limited to your typical retailer–wholesaler relationships, print and TV (as means of advertising); but now, the models have completely evolved from being D2C enabled and phygital to deploying influencers as a means of reaching the masses. For example, when Covid struck, people across India suddenly found themselves equipped with the tools to build their distribution networks through platforms like YouTube and Instagram. What had once been the exclusive domain of large brands with hefty marketing budgets was now open to anyone armed with creativity and a smartphone.

As traditional channels like TV and print struggled to maintain relevance during the lockdown, digital-first distribution emerged as the most effective way to reach consumers. Influencers, who had already established trust with their communities, became ideal partners for brands to collaborate with, as brands did not have to spend money or time to build this digital distribution firsthand.

Now let us talk about fashion, a sector where mastering distribution can make or break a brand. Fashion trends are changing and so are the choices of Gen Z. They are very conscious of their looks and appearance and picky about what they use and wear, including clothes, watches, smartphones, deodorants and perfumes.

One such fashion statement today, which involves looking down at other people's feet but can't be looked down upon in any way, is sneakers.

It is expected that in 2025, India's sneakers market will generate 3.1 billion dollars in revenue, which reflects the growing popularity of this category. Sneakers have become a status symbol, a style statement and sometimes even a collector's dream. In fact, these items have become so lucrative that there are entire courses in colleges dedicated to the business of shoes.

Now, we have already talked about how crucial distribution is in fashion, but in sneakers? That's a whole different story. You don't just launch sneakers; you drop them. Distribution here isn't just about filling shelves, it is about building hype. Limited-edition releases, celebrity collabs, sneaker flipping, exclusive pop-ups and whatnot are important nodes that characterize this space. Mastering this 'distribution' in sneakers means nailing the balance between being 'everywhere' yet making customers feel 'exclusive'.

This uniqueness of sneaker distribution models is what led us to getting inspired and to choose someone from the world of sneakers, mind you, a 'sneaker' himself, to share insights on cracking distribution in this fast-paced, ever-evolving digital era.

Distribution in Business Is Like the Circulation System in the Human Body

Just as blood flows through veins and arteries to deliver oxygen and nutrients to every part of the body, distribution channels ensure that products or services reach consumers at the right time and at the right place.

Having a product or a service to offer doesn't mean you have a business. You don't have a business unless you have distribution.

In the previous chapters, we placed a lot of emphasis on the technical mechanics of a startup, from the idea to the MVP to team-building, mentorship and even acquiring the first 100 customers, but we haven't talked about how to build pipelines to eventually scale your business. This chapter covers that.

How Does a Giant like HUL Distribute?

Without distribution, a business can't be built and profits can't come in. To illustrate this, let us take the example of Hindustan Unilever Limited (HUL).

HUL has consistently refined its distribution network to stay ahead in India's competitive market. Leveraging technologies like SAP, GPS tracking and data analytics, HUL achieved real-time stock visibility, optimized delivery routes and reduced both stockouts and fuel consumption.

Project Shakti played a key role in expanding HUL's reach, empowering over 1.9 lakh rural women entrepreneurs, known as Shakti Ammas, to become D2C distributors. This initiative has enabled HUL to penetrate more than 1 million villages, creating a cost-effective, sustainable distribution model. As a result, HUL boosted sales in underserved areas, improved stock turnover and cultivated stronger customer loyalty, all while fostering an entrepreneurial mindset among rural women.

Consequently, customer satisfaction and loyalty soared, cementing HUL's position as India's market leader in consumer goods.

So, with an effective distribution strategy, a company can:

1. Reach a Wider Audience
2. Enhance Convenience
3. Increase Sales and Revenue
4. Build Brand Awareness and Loyalty
5. Adapt to Changing Consumer Behaviour
6. Empower Communities

Distribution is evolving day in and day out. Every day, a new model or tweaks to existing models or technology come up. From physical layers to now online and technology-enabled layers, a lot has changed. As the world order changes, newer and newer business models have come up and will keep coming up.

Modern retail and D2C platforms are posing a threat to the family-run brick and mortar stores, and your '*paas wali kirane ki dukaan* [neighbourhood grocer]'. Offline gossip with the nearby store owner have turned into online gossip, taking the form of reviews, user-generated content and what not.

Now, coming back to sneakers, let us read the story of an entrepreneur who built one of the largest sneaker brands in India using modern forms of distribution.

This is the story of Vedant Lamba from Mainstreet Marketplace.

The Story of a 'Sneakerhead' Who Built a $9.89 Million Business

In 2017, a young boy named Vedant Lamba started a YouTube channel[2] and began uploading daily vlogs on it. One day, he came across an article on 'sneaker culture' and how it presented a new opportunity for Bharat. After reading the article, he became interested to know more about this space. He felt that as a category this space had the potential to explode. Vedant thought, 'This is pretty interesting. Why don't I read more about and explore this space further?'

Soon, he started researching this industry and its evolution. During this time, he noticed one gap. Though sneakers had already begun to take the world by storm, they had not yet drawn the attention of Bharat. There were shoes, but no major sneaker brands in the country. Armed with this insight, he decided to fill the gap. And so, he launched Mainstreet TV, a channel on YouTube,[3] through which he aimed to provide insights and educate consumers on what sneakers are and how they are going to be the next big thing. He started this activity with the goal of building a brand out of sneakers. Soon, he started gaining traction on Mainstreet's YouTube channel. It proved that people loved sneakers but had no accessibility to popular choices. He capitalized on the growth on YouTube by founding Mainstreet Marketplace, an online platform that rapidly became a go-to destination for sneaker enthusiasts.

Vedant's vision and hard work paid off as Mainstreet Marketplace became a go-to destination for sneakerheads nationwide. The platform offered a wide range of coveted brands like Yeezy, Jordan, Adidas, Nike, Drew House and Supreme, attracting customers from all walks of life, including Bollywood celebrities like Ranveer Singh and Ranbir Kapoor. But let us look at why this is an even bigger feat than what it looks like.

The Distribution of Sneakers

Distribution in the sneaker industry is very different from traditional retail products, which focus on mass production and wide availability.

In the world of sneakers, distribution is about creating a controlled scarcity that drives demand. Limited sneaker releases, often timed to perfection, are strategically designed to sell out fast. This fast-paced selling process not only heightens consumer desire but also adds an element of urgency that further fuels the hype.

Additionally, sneaker brands strategically implement tiered retail systems, ensuring that only select retailers receive high-demand models. This model enhances brand prestige, as the sneakers are often 'released' in limited quantities to a select group of high-end or specialty stores.

For instance, exclusive Jordan releases are typically reserved for specific stores. The scarcity of these items further drives up demand, with customers scrambling for a chance to secure a pair. Even, the sneaker community, or *sneakerheads*, plays a critical role in distribution. Their enthusiasm, loyalty, and social media presence amplify the brand's reach. When a sneaker drops, it's not just a product release, it's a full-blown event. Sneakers like Yeezys or limited-edition Nikes see immediate online buzz, with sneakerheads sharing their excitement across platforms like Instagram, Twitter and Reddit.

Their influence doesn't stop at retail and extends into the resale market, which can sometimes drive prices to astronomical levels. For example, a pair of limited-edition Air Jordans, originally priced at $200, can resell for over $1,000, making the secondary market a vital component of the overall distribution ecosystem. These exclusive retail experiences, combined with online drops, make the sneaker market one of the most dynamic and high-demand retail spaces.

A Purview of Distribution in the Traditional Business Sense

Now that we have looked into why distribution models are different in the sneaker industry, let us dive into what distribution truly means at its core.

One of the most important aspects of any distribution strategy is the intersection of pricing and the activeness of the ideal customer profile (ICP). The ICP refers to the specific segment of consumers who are most likely to purchase a product based on demographic, geographic and psychographic factors (as we also saw in the chapter on KYC).

A well-defined ICP allows a brand to align its distribution efforts with the preferences and purchasing behaviours of its most engaged consumers. Pricing (as we discussed in Boult's case) plays a pivotal role in this equation. Whether it's a luxury brand or a mass-market product, pricing and distribution must complement each other to maximize reach and profitability. For example, high-end luxury brands like Gucci or Rolex often employ exclusive distribution channels such as flagship stores, boutique locations or invitation-only releases. These channels create an aura of prestige and exclusivity, which resonates with their affluent and selective ICP.

On the other hand, mass-market grocery products like Coca-Cola or Nestlé are distributed through a much broader array of traditional retail channels, including supermarkets, convenience stores and e-commerce platforms. The target group for these products is far more general, focusing on consumers seeking convenience and affordability.

So, in a nutshell, ICP defines the customer; the customer establishes the price and the price drives up distribution. Distribution would drive up sales, which drives profits.

You have to credit us for summarizing this whole piece in a line. And it is not rocket science. Create a winning product that solves the customer's problem and one that is available at the right place and price; you will succeed. But that still leaves one final question that we want to answer for you:

Does That Mean if I Have the Right Product and Pricing, I Can Distribute It Anywhere?

Now, as distribution strategies are crafted, a key approach that brands use is to focus on mastering one platform or channel before expanding to others. This allows brands to optimize their operations and customer engagement tactics in a single, manageable space before diversifying. For example, Amazon focused on mastering its e-commerce platform before branching out into logistics, physical stores with Amazon Go and cloud services. This strategy of refining operations on one platform allows a brand to perfect its distribution model, which it can tweak and replicate to scale to other avenues.

Even when I, Surya, consult brands and startups, I always emphasize the importance of mastering one social media platform before jumping on to others. By doing so, you ensure that your foundation is solid and scalable. Once you have optimized one channel and fully understand your customer base, you will be in a much stronger position to expand to other platforms without losing focus or efficiency.

To conclude, we can say that the story of Vedant and sneakers gives us an insight into the important aspect of distribution. The takeaway lesson is that like Vedant, we need to keep our eyes open to details of any business if we have to identify the gaps and leverage them to our advantage, thereby insinuating into an already available market in a unique way and creating our own space. You need to literally sneak into the motherboard if you have to create a new interface on the visible screen of that business.

And yes, for that distribution is key!

So, What Should You Do Next?

List the platforms that you think would be the right fit for distributing your product or service. Rank them in order of importance for achieving your goals.

Also, like in the previous chapter, given below is the framework called RISING, which will guide you through Mainstreet Marketplace's journey in a nutshell:

Roadblock	**Ideal Customer**	**Solution**	**Innovation**	**Nakad (Money)**	**Growth**
Limited awareness and accessibility of premium sneaker brands Lack of platforms catering specifically to sneakerheads and enthusiasts in India Managing exclusive and limited releases amidst high demand and counterfeit concerns	Sneaker enthusiasts and fashion-forward individuals Tech-savvy Gen Z and Millennials	An online platform offering a curated selection of premium sneakers Ensuring genuine products through trusted reseller partnerships and verification processes	Leveraging YouTube and social media to educate and build a community around sneaker culture in India Partnering directly with global brands for unique launches and pop-up events	Product Sales through physical as well as online stores	Attracting diverse clientele including celebrities and influencers, cementing brand presence and loyalty Strengthening the sneakerhead community through engagement initiatives, fostering long-term customer relationships

12

Retaining Your Customer

Take from an AI Mobile Keyboard Company with 100 Million Users

Bobble AI[1] is an AI-powered super keyboard platform making smartphone interactions personalized, expressive and smarter with deep-tech innovations. Bobble AI is enhancing the creative expression and daily productivity of over 100 million users globally. It is the most engaged and the highest-rated keyboard platform in India. It supports 150 languages (including twenty-two official Indian languages). Users can convert text into visual elements like stickers, GIFs, emojis, custom fonts, etc. Stickers and GIFs can be personalized with the user's own face, expression and message. Users can leverage generative AI seamlessly across all apps/use cases on their smartphones directly from their Bobble AI keyboard.

Over 100 billion messages are sent every single day via WhatsApp and other messaging apps.

That's an astounding number, isn't it? But have you ever paused to think about what makes all this communication possible? Well, let's take a moment to think about it. What's that tool that enables us to send all these messages?

If you're still wondering, let us reveal the answer. It's the 'keyboard' on your smartphone. Yes! That tiny input software you use to type out everything, from entire conversations to emojis and stickers. It is the unglorified hero behind all our digital communication.

Now, let us ask you a question: 'What language do you use while texting someone?' Is it just one out of English, Hindi, Telugu, Malayalam, Bengali or Gujarati, or is it perhaps a mix of several of these languages? Though it may not be quite evident to you, most of us change the language when we talk to different people and blend languages and slang in our everyday conversations.

With our screen times increasing every single day, mobile keyboards have evolved significantly. Initially, we could only send simple text messages. But now, we can send GIFs, images, videos and even audio messages. Keyboards have become more interactivityity-driven than text-driven. Earlier, keyboards in Bharat were mostly open source, but some global companies like Google and Indian companies like Bobble AI have come up to innovate and disrupt the space. And, this is the company we approached for this chapter. Keyboards have also evolved from just being a communication tool to being a recommendation tool and a digital billboard (some of the recommendations on keyboards are sponsored by the advertisers). Bobble did many such sponsored advertisor campaigns including the one with Oreo.

Today, smartphone manufacturers are busy integrating generative AI capabilities directly into keyboard software, fundamentally reshaping how users interact with their devices.

Take Samsung, for instance—its Galaxy AI offers intelligent tone suggestions and rephrasing tools, allowing users to adjust the style and mood of their messages effortlessly, while also providing top-tier spelling and grammar corrections.

It's a great example of how even something as simple as a *keyboard* can ride the wave of innovation. Everyday tools we barely notice are being transformed by advanced technology. In India, this knack for creative problem-solving is often referred to as *jugaad*—resourceful, cost-effective solutions born out of necessity.

This brings us to Bobble AI. How did they turn something as humble as a keyboard into an innovation that reached over **100 million users**—roughly **one in eight smartphone users** globally? More importantly, in a world where users can easily jump to the next flashy app, how did Bobble AI ensure they didn't fall victim to the dreaded *leaky bucket syndrome* (losing users faster than they gain new ones)?

Retention is crucial for any startup—scaling without retention is like trying to fill a bucket with a hole at the bottom. Bobble AI not only scaled rapidly but managed to retain users by constantly innovating, engaging their audience and solving real user pain points. To truly understand how they did it, we need to delve into the journey of **Ankit**

Prasad, co-founder of Bobble AI, and explore the strategies that helped them sustain growth over time.

From a Small Town to Building a Company Worth $142 Million

Ankit hails from Chaibasa, a small town in Jharkhand. In 1997, his father, driven by a vision of the future, established a computer centre in Chaibasa, a place where computers were virtually unknown. Ankit's upbringing in a humble and modest family meant that having a computer at home was a privilege. It was like a gateway to dreams and one that ignited his early passion for technology.

Ankit started getting really passionate about computers at a young age. He delved into programming, experimenting with tools like Logo and Basic. By the time he was in his teens, Ankit had become proficient at coding, earning recognition in his local community as a bright young coder.

During the interview, Ankit recalled, 'My father was a laboratory in-charge at a local college in Chaibasa that time. He was a visionary father, who later became professor at NIT Jamshedpur. He taught us so many good lessons about how the world is going to shape up in the new world of internet and computers. I developed a passion for computers at the age of four or five. Logo became one of my favorite tools. It's one of the earliest software which was used to command a cursor that moved forward five steps, and then BASIC became my first programming language. With the help of Logo and MS Paint, I remember I had created the Indian flag, the one who used it was the district collector who did flag hoisting on the 15th of August. I gained some popularity in the local region that this kid seems to be a bright coder. That's how my passion for coding began at the age of six.'

Getting into IIT Delhi and Launching His First Startup

Ankit worked really hard for his IIT exams and managed to secure an admission into the prestigious IIT Delhi. But life had other plans for him. He and his brother developed 'TouchTalent' in their dorm room in 2012, after being inspired by the achievements of Flipkart, Snapdeal and Zomato. It was envisioned as a social network in 2011, before Instagram was even born. Their vision was to create a platform for the creative community to collaborate, share their creativity with the world and monetize their talents.

But they were probably in the wrong place at the wrong time. It didn't work out the way they had expected. There was one major reason for their failure. They expanded too soon, which helped them achieve milestones like having a million artists from 100 countries on the platform. However, they realized that aiming for users from so many countries was not the most effective strategy. Instead, it only fragmented their user base, hindering their ability to monetize and benefit from the network effect.

But you see, Ankit was an astute entrepreneur. He didn't take failure as a setback. Instead, he used the lessons he learnt later on in their entrepreneurial journey.

From TouchTalent to Bobble AI

While TouchTalent didn't work out the way they wanted it to, Ankit and his brother Rahul consciously chose to keep the same legal entity for their next venture, Bobble

AI. Although they had the option to switch entities and stakeholders, they believed that people who support you in the early days need to be given their due for their contribution and loyalty, by retaining them in your team and giving them the value that they deserve.

Their previous company TouchTalent was predominantly web-based, which they had realized was a weak point. So, how did Ankit and his brother turn their weakness into building a multi-million-dollar business? To be precise, a USD 142 million-dollar keyboard business?[2]

Well, by the latter half of 2014, they began critically questioning whether their web-based platform would be acceptable to mobile users, especially given that in India, mobile penetration was occurring much more rapidly than web penetration. In a country like India, one couldn't expect people to afford laptops and desktops as smartphones were becoming increasingly affordable. Even instant messaging apps like Hike, Viber and WhatsApp were gaining popularity rapidly.

Faced with these challenges, they revisited the drawing board. They had to choose between two things—decide whether to force-fit the web-based creative social network into a mobile format or rethink their approach entirely. With some primary and secondary research, they realized that people primarily bought smartphones for two reasons. First to converse with others through texts and social media and second to take pictures. Most of the time, the buyer's decision was based on the quality of the camera embedded in the smartphone and its overall functionality. This insight was a pivotal starting point for blending their technological and creative strengths into Bobble.

Now, given their DNA, they decided to revisit their approach. Over weeks and months of contemplating and their past experiences with TouchTalent made them realize that integrating conversation and camera features could be their unique proposition. This led to the creation of their first product, which they called 'Bobble Comic Stories'. It allowed users to create comic stories using their selfies, turning them into bobblehead characters. Despite the initial version being rudimentary, it went viral because of its novel concept.

The virality coefficient of this product was so high that by 2015, they were adding a million users every couple of months to the entire Bobble App. But with virality, they also started to notice some major flaws. The experience of generating and sharing content within chat apps and social platforms was just cumbersome. Users had to leave their conversations to create content, save it and then share it with their friends and family.

So, Bobble had to do something about it. They thought of something innovative, which no one had done at the time. They thought, 'Why not create a small circular widget that appears on top of WhatsApp?' This hack allowed users to seamlessly create and share content without leaving the conversation. Users loved it so much that it significantly boosted Bobble's virality. It became so popular that many competitors copied their features, which the team took as an endorsement of their direction. Ankit recalls, 'Merely copying a feature does not guarantee success, and many of those who replicated our approach eventually failed.'

Execution is what matters in entrepreneurship. Business is execution. You could give ten million-dollar ideas to people out there for free, but maybe only one or none would succeed in actually creating a business worth that much.

By late 2015, Bobble AI faced another roadblock when Android OS removed the API that allowed their widget to function. This disruption forced them to rethink how to maintain the seamless flow of content sharing. Fortunately, around the same time, Android and iOS introduced third-party keyboard APIs. This development signaled a new opportunity to them.

Now, coming back to the story again, Ankit remembers, 'During those times, our engineering team was always exploring what was new in the market. For example, there was the Facebook Graph API, which we were the first to adopt in India. When third-party keyboard APIs were introduced by Android and iOS, we were the first to grab it and build a keyboard, primarily with the intent of integrating content inside the keyboard and bringing back the seamlessness of content sharing that was missing due to the disappearance of the widget.' It allowed users to share stickers and GIFs directly within their conversations, restoring the seamless experience they had initially created. Bobble's keyboard was a pioneer in bringing such functionality to the market.

When they ventured into the keyboard space, Ankit and his team quickly noticed that while the concept of content sharing was appreciated, the keyboard experience itself was lagging. You see, the keyboard was a complex product to build. Initially, they used some open-source code to test their hypothesis, however, they only faced rejection of their hypothesis. Their overall keyboard experience and user feedback were not positive. Users were unhappy with the product, as reflected in the poor ratings, and it was not growing as their content widget had.

Using Data to Decipher Customers' Needs and Wants and Eventually Retaining Them

If you are an entrepreneur, you need to learn from data. There is simply no way around it.

On the surface, the story might look very different from reality. The reality was that people loved the concept of content sharing via a keyboard, but they hated the typing experience. Therefore, Bobble had to make it a priority to solve the keyboard typing experience for the Indian geography and Indic languages. For the next two years, they eagerly worked on fixing the Indic language typing and voice-based speech-to-text experience, aiming to become the most engaging and highest retaining keyboard for Bharat.

During this time, Google introduced a separate Indic keyboard, but it later consolidated with Gboard, aiming to set a global standard.[3] However, feedback from thousands of users revealed that while they loved the Google Indic keyboard experience, they did not like Gboard because it was not built for India. It was built for the world.

As luck would have it, this presented a once-in-a-lifetime opportunity for Ankit, Rahul and their team—they created a mobile Indic keyboard tailored to the unique needs of Indian users. This move helped them regain user trust and improve the keyboard experience while maintaining superior content-sharing capabilities.

From 2016 to 2018, the team adamantly dedicated two years to fixing the keyboard experience. They understood that this factor was hindering their growth. By getting into the depths of the problem, they realized that people wanted to type in their native language. However, one unique insight they had over Gboard was that the new generation did not talk in the native script. They used a mix of dialects, often typing native language words using the Latin alphabet (for example: K-Y-A, space, K-A-R, space, R-A-H-A, for 'kya kar raha').

This insight, missed by larger players like Google, became the core of Bobble's development. The challenge was that this 'macaronic version' of the language had no fixed grammar or spelling, making it a freehand linguistic phenomenon with no official resources to build upon. This lack of standardization became their advantage.

Additionally, they realized that users often switched off the auto-correct function on their default keyboards because it never worked for their needs. This insight helped them understand that an amazing product like Microsoft SwiftKey was limited to English-speaking knowledge workers and could not penetrate real Bharat.

Competing with Google and Partnering with Xiaomi

Despite continuing challenges, from 2016 to 2019, Bobble AI's user base remained relatively flat. Many VCs rejected them. The key reason for this was their inability to answer one single question: How would you compete with Google? This answer came to Ankit in 2019, when he was attending a guest lecture at Harvard University. The lecture was on the 'Incumbent's Dilemma'. It was an interesting and exciting concept that made Ankit think.

The 'Incumbent's Dilemma' theory describes that a large player in a playground, occupying a major chunk of it, has set his own rules and regulations. If a new entrant tries to play against that player in the same playground, they are bound to lose. This was the mistake everyone, including Ankit and his team, was making.

Bobble needed to create their own playground with their own rules. This was basically offering OEMs (Original Equipment Manufacturers) a completely customized product suited to their specific brand, model and target audience, without restricting access to user data. Other players used to give OEMs a black box and paid them upfront to enable their system in mobile devices. This was an anti-thesis to what Google was doing. Ankit went back, called his team for a 'town hall' and discussed what he had learnt at Harvard. They then decided to create a co-branded product, whilst sharing user data, and to offer revenue-sharing in a transparent manner.

This strategy led them to convince smaller OEMs and later Xiaomi, which became their partner and investor in 2019, leading to their explosive growth. From 2019 onwards, Xiaomi's partnership became the tipping point, allowing Bobble to grow massively.

But now that they had acquired a large user base, it was very important for them to retain users as well. After all, if you are not retaining your customers, you are not building a business.

How Did Bobble AI Retain 100 Million+ Users?

Bobble's user acquisition features are different from user retention features. Ankit advises against instantly gratifying the users on the app. Even if you create many loops and products, if the user motivation is high, they will take any number of steps to complete the task at hand. During onboarding, they make users chat with a bubbly assistant. This gives out the user intent and behaviour. Retention comes when you use those learnings in real time to present users with an interface they like.

As Ankit puts it:

> There are a few features that enable our users to stay or at least encourage them to stay for a few days. This is how you solve retention in steps. You don't aim for ninety-day retention on day one. First, you want to ensure that if a user comes, all necessary data is provided. Initially, we admit we are unsure of the future, and it might take two or three minutes to address that uncertainty. This initial engagement of two or three minutes can extend to seven days, and then we aim for the user to stay for at least thirty days.
>
> To achieve this, we use strategies like targeting power users, who are the most active users. For increased usage, we implement state machine notifications and other strategies. Our product falls into a generic category; it is an essential smartphone product that

anyone can use. Customization according to user needs is crucial. As an investor, you may have different expectations from your smartphone experience, and thus your keyboard experience should add value to that. However, a student, retailer or rickshaw driver might have different expectations, and the keyboard should enhance their smartphone experience with a custom interface and features.

The speed at which the product identifies who you are and delivers the relevant functionalities and interface are what the product manager should focus on. Quickly gathering data from the consumer and adapting the interface accordingly is vital for retention. In our case, user quality is paramount because our product is sensitive, used over 100 times a day. Whether playing games, chatting or making transactions, a keyboard crash or lag is unacceptable as it ruins the experience. Hence, our default assumption for retention is 100 per cent. Any negative incident could lead to a loss of users, making retention a critical focus.

We must prevent negative incidents from happening in the future. Identifying and addressing such incidents ensures that they don't recur. Within our platform, we have several layers aimed at different objectives. The first layer focuses on hygiene, ensuring a smooth typing experience. Issues like lag, unresponsiveness or crashes harm user experience. We have a dedicated team continuously working on this.

The second layer is expression, which includes various kinds of content like different fonts, movie dialogues, trailers, songs, news, jokes and quotes.

The third layer is recommendations, ranging from app recommendations to products and services. Misidentifying user intent can damage trust. For instance, if someone writes 'Love you, Papa', and the keyboard suggests something inappropriate, it can hurt the user experience. We aim to avoid such mistakes by understanding user intent better

Organic growth has worked well for us, mainly through content sharing. Every piece of content shared carries a watermark, helping us penetrate user networks. We also post daily video stories that users make their status messages. Each status has a video and a link, drawing in new users from those who view these statuses.

All that is fine, but does that mean if you charge every step of the way, it affects retention?

To this Ankit says:

Well, yes. You need to be careful. Monetization is crucial for growth, but if you charge everywhere, it can overwhelm users and lead to higher churn rates. The challenge is finding the right balance.

Regarding monetization, it must be carefully balanced with user retention. Aggressive monetization can harm user experience and retention, as seen with platforms like YouTube and Facebook. If monetization is too intrusive or frequent, users may feel frustrated and disengage.

We aim to monetize without hurting the user experience. For example, platforms like SonyLIV show ads before allowing users to continue watching a show.

While ads are a common form of monetization, they can be disruptive if overused. We strive for a monetization strategy that maintains user engagement and retention, ensuring sustainable growth without compromising the user experience.

Is Retention Random or Is There a Strategy Behind It?

Retention indeed is a science. Every company faces churn and uninstalls happen *rozana* (every day). The real challenge lies in minimizing this churn and keeping users engaged over time. So, how do companies scientifically approach retention? Are there any proven principles or frameworks they follow?

Well, one of the most used tools for understanding retention is cohort analysis. By tracking user behaviour over specific time intervals—like D10 (day 10) or D30 (day 30) after installation, companies can identify patterns and spot the drop-off points. This analysis helps in answering two critical questions:

1. How many users are still active after ten days?
2. Are users finding enough value to return after thirty days?

In order to track retention effectively, businesses define North Star metrics—the key indicators that reflect the product's core value. These metrics differ from industry to industry, for example:

1. In a social app, it might be the number of active chats per user, or the number of posts liked or average view duration per reel by category.
2. In a SaaS product, it could be the number of key features used within the first week.
3. For a gaming app, it might be tied to the number of levels completed or daily logins and in-app purchases.

Never on your way to retaining your customers, assume that simply measuring a few metrics will be enough to retain your customers. Retention tracking is never just about numbers, it's also about identifying the moments when users experience value and ensuring they reach those moments consistently. The onus is on us entrepreneurs, to run experiments to improve or maintain these metrics, like nudging users back through notifications, improving the onboarding experience or offering personalized content.

Now, here's a fun fact: while Instagram was the most downloaded app in 2023, it was also the most deleted app of the same year. We hope that after reading this, you'll pay a little more attention to retention.

Also, if you are as curious as we are to dive deeper into the world of retention, feel free to check out the blog links attached in the notes.[4]

Key Takeaways

- **Be Pioneering:** Identifying future trends early, as Ankit's father did with computers in the late 1990s, can provide a significant first-mover advantage to you as entrepreneurs.

- **Not Just Viral:** Businesses should not just focus on acquiring users through viral features but ensure a seamless and valuable product experience.
- **Execution Is Key:** Great ideas alone are not enough. Execution is what builds businesses. Even if you have a million-dollar idea, success comes from how well you execute it and adapt based on feedback.
- **Go Local:** Businesses should localize their offerings to fit the cultural and linguistic needs of their customers.
- **Retain, Retain, Retain:** Acquiring customers is important but retaining them is critical for sustainable business growth.
- **Partner Up:** Strategic partnerships with larger players in the ecosystem can provide businesses with access to new audiences and resources they wouldn't have on their own.

So, What Should You Do Next?

Brainstorm on five exclusive content ideas that would delight your customers or prospects and write them down in the space given below.

Also, like in the previous chapter, given below is the framework called RISING, which will guide you through Bobble AI's journey in a nutshell:

Roadblock	**Ideal Customer**	**Solution**	**Innovation**	**Nakad (Money)**	**Growth**
Intense competition from players like Google	Any smartphone user in India, but mostly in the age group of 18 to 35	Created a mobile Indic keyboard tailored to Indian languages Integrated content sharing within the keyboard Personalized keyboard experience based on user data and preferences	Developed a widget for seamless content sharing Customized keyboard for each OEM, sharing user data and revenue transparently	Revenue through customized keyboard solutions and partnerships	Partnering with Xiaomi in 2019 Integrating third-party APIs

13

Bootstrapping Versus Fundraising

Multimillion-Dollar Exit and Raising Funds from Founders of CRED, Paytm and Mamaearth

Crib is India's no. 1 property management app that helps landlords, property managers and co-living operators automate rent collection, streamline tenant onboarding and manage operations effortlessly. Trusted by over 2500 landlords and managing 2,00,000-plus units, Crib transforms property management with real-time analytics, smart billing and white-labelled tenant apps. Backed by Rebright Partners, FAAD Capital, WeFounderCircle and over fifty marquee angels like the founders of Cred, Paytm, Droom, BharatPe, Mamaearth, etc. Sunny Garg and Shaifali Jain, co-founders of Crib, also started YourShell,[1] a full-stack co-living operator while in college. After three years of operations and a turnover of over Rs 20 crore, it was sold at a multi-million-dollar valuation to Stanza Living. In Crib, they were later joined by their third co-founder, Archit Chauhan, who is also their CTO.

Zoho and Zerodha, or Zepto and Zomato—do you know what is common among them, apart from the letter Z? They are some of the biggest, path-breaking startups in India.

But still, there is one thing that sets them apart.

While Zoho and Zerodha are bootstrapped companies with Rs 0 in external capital raised from funds, Zepto and Zomato are massively funded, raising USD 3.6 billion.

Now, what even is bootstrapping and fundraising? Well, keep reading to find out.

In the last chapter we explored how to retain your startup's customers and develop product stickiness. Establishing a loyal customer base is undoubtedly crucial for the success of any business. Satisfied customers not only provide recurring revenue but also act as brand ambassadors, helping to attract new customers through positive word-of-mouth.

Your startup could have different customer groups, each with varied needs and preferences (we looked at this in the chapter on KYC). For a startup, this group further translates to recurring revenue (money), the foundation upon which a startup can grow and thrive sustainably. You want to open a restaurant—you need money. And then you need more to buy raw materials, tables, chairs, cutlery and so much more.

But think of this—what if your restaurant gets 5000 orders daily?

That's amazing, right? But hold on, growth and expansion require more fund. You'll need money to hire extra hands to serve all those customers, maybe expand your floor space and invest in advanced equipment to meet the demand.

So, the question is—where will all this money come from? Well, there are primarily two sources to it. Bootstrapping and 'fundraising'.

What Do Bootstrapping and Fundraising Mean?—A Fun Example

Bootstrapping is when you ask for capital (money) from your friends and family. Maybe you remember asking your dad or mom for pocket money during your childhood? That is bootstrapping because you are raising funds from internal investors who would not ask for it to be returned. You have no pressure to return the money; you can use it on your terms and basically become self-sustainable. And your parents wouldn't even bother to ask questions before giving you the pocket money because they know you.

Let's switch gears in the example a bit, what if you had gotten your pocket money from the bank? The bank would make you file various loan documents and demand identification proofs. They would also underwrite and see whether you are eligible for the money. This is raising funds from external sources, which falls under the fundraising category.

These external sources encompass a spectrum of avenues, from angel investors, venture capitalists, private equity and venture debt professionals. Some notable examples of successful funded startups in India are OYO Rooms, BharatPe, Digit Insurance, Groww, Dream11 and many others.

Now that we have already talked about why money for your startup is essential, let's step into the boots of someone who first ran a successful bootstrapped startup, exited it and then stepped back into building another startup, but this time, one where he was able to successfully raise funds from the likes of Vijay Shekhar Sharma from Paytm and Ghazal Alagh from Mamaearth.

Meet Sunny Garg and Shaifali Jain, the duo behind YourShell (bootstrapped), now joined by Archit Chauhan at Crib (funded).

For the purpose of this chapter, we picked the brains of Sunny Garg.

From a Middle-Class Family in Delhi to Co-Founding Two Successful Startups

Despite being born in a middle-class family, Sunny's ambitions were high-class (we mean first-class). *Sapne uunche dekhta thha woh!* He tried starting various ventures in his college, but despite his best attempts, he failed. Despite those failures, tinkering with ideas became his second nature. Due to this, opportunities started popping up in front of him. Yes, he had spent so much time on the ground during his days at Ramjas College, Delhi University, that opportunities started looking for him instead of him looking for opportunities.

When the admissions season began at his college, he noticed one common concern among both parents and students. '*Yaar, rehne ki accha jagah kaha milegi, bees jagah ja chuke hai, but zyadatar places bahut gandi hai and kuch amenities and safety bhi nahi hai* [where will we find a good place to live, we have been to twenty places now and almost all places are dirty with no amenities or safety].' He also noticed that students were struggling with their admission formalities.

Hearing these concerns, Sunny had a 'light-bulb moment'. He thought why not help students with their admission formalities and in turn also help them find accommodation. After all, he faced the same issue while he was looking for accommodation, too. So, he started right away and approached the parents and students and promised to help them find accommodation. Initially, he launched an initiative called *HailDU*, and within just twenty-three days, he managed to help 400 students find accommodation. He went door to door to explain to paying guest (PG) and hostel owners about what he was trying to build. The business model was simple: charge landlords 5–7 per cent of their revenue. However, Sunny soon realized that many landlords were not providing good service, leading to dissatisfaction among students. That's when he decided to launch *YourShell*, a solution that focused not just on finding housing but also on ensuring a high-quality living experience. At *YourShell*, the model evolved: take properties on lease, furnish them, and provide essential services before renting them out to students. The PG and hostel owners liked his proposition and saw value in offering a standardized, well-managed living experience through the platform.

But then challenges started to rise. Students used to keep calling him: '*Bhaiya laundry nahi hai, khana nahi hai* [there is no laundry or food service here].' Sunny realized this and started building his team to carefully address these issues. Soon, what began as a journey in 2017 with a young twenty-year-old college boy was able to flourish into a successful business, leaving a mark.

But does that mean his journey was easy? Didn't he try to raise money? He did, but people used to give him goal-based targets. 'Sunny, you only have eighteen beds right now, make it 100 and then you will get funding.' When he reached 100 beds, people would say, 'Sunny you only have 100 beds right now, make it 250 and then you will get funding.' He achieved that number as well and kept expanding and growing more. But still, he didn't get any funding. Despite being rejected by countless VCs and investors, he continued on.

And you need to, too. Failing doesn't make you weak. It only gives you the courage to keep pushing and learn from your mistakes.

Despite these rejections from investors, YourShell, became a brand which was much appreciated for delivering a robust service support system for handling student grievances along with an exciting array of value-added features, including a library, gaming zone, career counseling sessions and internship guidance. It was also among the youngest startups to raise venture debt under the Government of India's 'Startup India' programme.

However, after building YourShell for a couple of years, Sunny and Shaifali got a great acquisition offer. Sunny recalls, 'At that time, we went nuts—we were simply amazed. In our early twenties, getting such a big multi-crore offer felt unreal. We thought our life was sorted—*ab toh sirf party karenge*!'

But their bootstrap journey was not easy at all. Even surviving every day was a challenge. So, let's give you a ringside view of an actual bootstrapping case.

What Did It Really Mean to Bootstrap YourShell?

Sunny's bootstrap journey started with a Rs 35 lakh loan (later increased to Rs 65 lakh) from Startup India, Standup India scheme of the Government of India. But the 35 lakhs were insufficient to run such a capital-intensive business as YourShell. So, he started taking loans from friends, customers, suppliers and the unorganized market.

The loans started with a rate of interest of 10 per cent p.a. (the government one), and as he moved to the outer circle, these rates increased.

For example, close friends gave loans at 12 per cent, distant friends at 18 per cent, customers and suppliers at 24 per cent, and this went even up to 48 per cent p.a. in case of emergencies. The average interest rate was 25 per cent p.a., and the total loan amount was Rs 4 crore in the final year.

Despite such debt piling up, he remained profitable and maintained a heads-up. However, it was challenging to run and manage everyday operations. Let us corroborate that with another instance from YourShell's days.

One day, a fake 'electricity team' raided his property. Inexperienced, he panicked and paid ₹60,000 as a fine, thinking the issue was resolved. Two days later, the same fake team hit another property. A local brought in a real officer, and the scammers vanished. But the real officials fined them ₹4.5 lakhs for the same problem.

All of this happened because of one small mistake.

In the properties where there were commercial metres, if the electricity bill monthly was an average of Rs 4 lakh per month, the collection was only Rs 3 lakh, making a loss every month. Sunny made a mistake to avoid a loss and continue operations without tenants leaving. The pressure of bootstrapping sometimes doesn't let you do things that should have been done first.

So, yes, he deserved every bit of the party when he sold YourShell to Stanza living for multi-million dollars.

I (Aditya Arora) have seen his journey first-hand as we continued to be the two most-spoken-about entrepreneurs in Delhi University circuit during that time.

Once an Entrepreneur, Always an Entrepreneur

Sunny and Shaifali had certainly been bitten by the entrepreneurial bug as they still wanted to solve problems in the property and real-estate market. But they wanted to do it differently this time and on a much larger scale.

They knew that YourShell was an asset-heavy model, something investors had frequently pointed out. So, they decided to build something more asset-light this time. They also did not want to make the mistakes that they had committed earlier—trying to build technology in-house, which wasn't their core. This time, they would rely on freelancers or consulting firms to build it.

After taking a break for a couple of years following their exit, Sunny and Shaifali dove into starting their new venture, Crib.

From YourShell to Crib: A Different Ball Game But the Same Field

At Crib, they aimed to create an enterprise powered by a tech product (with Archit Chauhan as their CTO), solving problems for landlords, service professionals and tenants.

Technology, as we discussed in the chapter on 'Expand My Business', helps you scale. Without it, you can only reach a limited set of customers and expand your business to a certain point. But with tech, you can scale faster without needing physical asset recovery. Recovery happens from Day 1.

All this technology was created at Crib by understanding the customer first-hand at YourShell.

Landlords spent hours sending rent reminders each month. So they automated it. Collecting payments from different modes was complicated. So they integrated the gateway into the Crib app and provided a user-friendly interface for making payments. With a vision to create an all-in-one property management application, they have already created wonders.

Crib is trusted by over 2500 landlords and managing 2,00,000-plus units (350x of what they could achieve at YourShell). And this time, they have already raised capital from 100-plus investors and eight unicorn founders.

So, Is Fundraising Better than Bootstrapping?

While we were having a chat over a cup of chai with Sunny, he said one thing on fundraising that we thought would make a lot of sense here.

Don't chase funding.

While funding seems glamorous, it gets you covered in the media and makes you an overnight celebrity. Don't chase funding.

Raise funds only when you are clear of what you can do with the funds. Raise funds only when you have a solid plan to utilize the funding and grow the company faster than ever before, maintaining some sort of a plan to give the money back to the investor. Or as in startup parlance, when you have a clear exit strategy.

While explaining this point for anyone looking to raise funds, Sunny (as always) came up with some other great punchlines.

1. **Never take the virginity of an investor.** Yes, it might sound provocative, but Sunny's point will become clear upon closer examination. He emphasized the caution entrepreneurs should exercise when engaging with angel investors, particularly those who are new to this form of investment and might not fully comprehend its intricacies. Give a realistic view to investors, even more to first-time investors and make them understand that their investment is not assured. It involves high-risk and return.
2. **Don't take the entire amount from one investor.** For this, Sunny, Shaifali and Archit demarcated their responsibilities very clearly, which resulted in them getting together eight unicorn founders, Jaipur's biggest builders, Kota's leading hostel owners, one of Lucknow's most prominent families, Ahmedabad's top CAs, and some of the biggest fintech founders in the country as investors.
3. **Never be the entire investment for any particular investor.** Diversification is important.

But What Is Better: Bootstrap or Funding?

Frankly, the answer is BOTH. It depends on business, ambitions, scalability and operational efficiency. While fundraising gives significant capital for growth, access to unparalleled mentorship and lots of glamour and marketing, it comes with a dilution of ownership and a certain intent to grow faster and return the capital of investors with a premium in three to five years. (As it should be).

Similarly, while bootstrapping gives greater control, more hands-on internal management and processes, it comes with a challenge of limited resources, crunched cash operating cycles and slower growth in formative years.

So, choose your own path depending upon your growth ambitions, market and propensity to scale rapidly. Both have their own limitations and advantages and there is no RIGHT choice.

The reason we chose Sunny, Shaifali and Archit for this chapter was to show that bootstrapping and funding have been both success stories at YourShell and Crib, respectively. The onus is on you to deliver! But wait . . .

Our simulation is only half done. In case you do decide to raise funds, hop on to the next chapter for a special surprise. Come soon, we are waiting!

Key Takeaways

- **Understand your customers' needs:** Different customer groups have varying needs, and understanding these differences is crucial for sustainable growth and recurring revenue.
- **Seek Self-Sustainability:** Before seeking external funding, ensure your business can sustain itself financially.

So, What Should You Do Next?

Take Rs 100 from your pocket (or your parents). Try to survive on this Rs 100 for a week. This will teach you the art of Bootstrapping!

Also, like in the previous chapter, given below is the framework called RISING, which will guide you through YourShell's and Crib's journey in a nutshell:

Roadblock	Ideal Customer	Solution	Innovation	Nakad (Money)	Growth
YourShell: Difficulty in finding clean and safe accommodations for students Managing operations, addressing student grievances, and achieving scalability without external funding **Crib:** Solving problems in the property and real-estate market on a larger scale, requiring significant capital and technology integration	**YourShell:** Students and parents looking for reliable, safe and clean accommodations near college campuses\. **Crib:** Landlords and tenants seeking a tech-driven solution to streamline rental processes and improve the rental experience	**YourShell:** Created standardized, clean and safe accommodations with added amenities such as a library, gaming zone, career counselling sessions and internship guidance **Crib:** Developed a tech product aimed at building a digital ecosystem to redefine landlord operations and enhance tenant experiences	**YourShell:** Developed a robust service support system to handle student grievances efficiently and provide value-added services **Crib:** Developed an asset-light model and leveraged technology to create scalable solutions for the property and real estate market, similar to the impact of Moore's Law in tech growth	**YourShell:** 15–20% of rent as profit **Crib:** Small fees from the operator	**YourShell:** Aimed at large-scale impact and exponential growth through technology **Crib:** Introducing SaaS offerings and white-label solutions

14

A Rookie's Guide to Raising Funds

A Special Investor's Take

In the previous chapter on Bootstrapping vs Fundraising, we explored how crucial 'capital' is to startups. In relation to startups, Bharat is at a unique and a bright position. The country is reforming with significant growth not only in the number of startups but also the number of investors, VCs and institutional funds. As per a report by Inc42,[1] total capital inflow in Indian startups as funding is estimated to touch USD 170 billion by 2025. This speaks a lot about how investors have been believing in the Bharat story. Also, the Indian Startup Ecosystem is on track to create 130 unicorns by 2025. Now, how better to hear about this topic than through the words of an investor themself.

Throughout this book, we have given you a glimpse of each step and phase of the entrepreneurial journey via each chapter. But the time has come to give you all a surprise through this chapter of the book. It is going to be special for two reasons. Firstly, we will be covering what entrepreneurship is and means through the investor's perspective. We will be talking about the different topics such as how to find investors for your startup, how to approach them, what to include in your pitch, how to assess the amount of funding you need at a particular stage for your startup, how to value your startup and so much more. And secondly, this chapter will be special for me, Surya Pasricha, in that I didn't have to toil hard to find a renowned investor for the interview. This investor is none other than my co-author, Aditya Arora, CEO of Faad Network. I told him: '*Aap bhi toh isi space mein ho and kaafi saare startups mein invest kar chuke ho. Kyun na aap hi iss topic pe light shed kar do?* [You are also in this space and have invested in several startups. Why don't you only shed light on this topic?].' Aditya agreed. Thereafter, we brainstormed as to which questions related to investing, funding, etc., would be important to answer for the young, first-time founders and which would be relevant to help them in their journey of startups.

We came up with the following questions:

1. Where do you find investors?
2. How to evaluate if an investor is the right one for your startup?
3. What to do after finding the right investor?
4. How to pitch to investors?
5. How to assess the amount of funding you need at a particular stage?
6. What do you need to provide to the investor on your cold message being accepted? What documents are required?

7. How many rounds does an entrepreneur have to go through to convince an investor?
8. Should you raise funding from one investor or multiple investors?
9. How do your value your startup?
10. Some dos and don'ts of pitching.

During our initial rounds of discussion, we were still pondering over whether we should cover this chapter or not and if yes, then how to do so. We realized that there was not enough material available on this topic. But the topic is highly relevant for a young entrepreneur.

FAAD Capital has invested in more than 100 startups, including companies like BluSmart, New Shop, Battery Smart, Hosteller and Grip Invest.

This is what he answered to the questions above.

1. Where Do You Find Investors?

In this digital era, one can find investors by keeping an eye out for something called 'demo days', where entrepreneurs like you get to pitch their ideas to potential investors. These events are gold mines for making connections. Also, one could use platforms like LinkedIn and X for reaching out to investors. In fact, some entrepreneurs have successfully landed investments by directly engaging with investors on X (formerly Twitter). So, put yourself out there and start connecting with potential backers online. You can also leverage online resources like startup databases and investor lists.

Websites like Startup India and media platforms such as YourStory and Inc42 Media often publish lists of top investors in the industry. Use these resources to identify potential investors and reach out to them with your pitch. Lastly, referrals can be a game-changer. If you know other founders who have successfully secured funding, ask them for introductions to their investors. Warm referrals carry a lot of weight in the startup world and can significantly increase your chances of getting noticed.

2. How to Evaluate If an Investor Is the Right One for Your Startup?

Firstly, understanding the investor is the key and for that you have to do in-depth research. This research entails going through their background, startups they have invested in before, taking feedback from other entrepreneurs building in the same space and more. You can also learn about them through their social media handles and by researching the performances of the startups in which they have invested.

The second way is to directly engage with the investor. Know their interest in investing in your venture, what they expect from the investment with you and in what ways they can contribute to the initial stages are key. What are their terms and conditions for the investment.

3. What To Do After Finding the Right Investor?

Finding the investor is just the initial step. Making them believe in you and funding your startup is another game altogether. It is all about building rapport, establishing trust and demonstrating the value of your venture. You have to date your fiancé for a few months before making them your spouse!

Start by getting to know potential investors and understanding their interests, preferences and investment criteria. Take the time to research investors and learn what they're looking for in a startup. Engage with investors through networking events, industry conferences and online platforms. Strike up conversations, share your story and listen to their feedback.

Remember, investors get pitched to frequently by a vast number of entrepreneurs. Hence, don't get discouraged in case they are not able to give you an audience initially. It may not be easy to get an appointment with them, so you need to be patient and persistent till you get to meet them.

Once you get a chance to pitch to them, be precise, clear and honest in showcasing the value of your startup and demonstrating your plan, resources and team to materialize your startup including the management of the investment amount you desire. Basically, you have to convince the investor that your pitch will give them good returns on their investment.

4. How to Pitch to Investors?

To get the best answer to this question, I felt it would help to know what the investor is looking at to choose the right startup for their investment. This would indirectly tell me what approach the entrepreneurs should adopt while pitching investors for a thumbs up. So, I posed this question to Aditya and specifically enquired, 'You must be receiving a lot of pitches on LinkedIn. How do you basically filter out which startup is the right one for you? Is there any kind of a message template that particularly intrigues investors, or what exactly is that last point you look out for?'

His response verbatim, is as follows.

Firstly, avoid sending blank messages or generic requests like, 'Hey, I'm looking to connect for funding.' This type of message doesn't distinguish itself and fails to provide any meaningful insight for the investor. It's a common occurrence in the entrepreneurial world, but it doesn't help you stand out.

Responding to generic messages doesn't provide any clear direction for the conversation. When reaching out to investors, it's essential to craft a message that offers more than just a pitch.

A good message template begins with a brief introduction that goes beyond just stating your company's name. Share a bit about yourself, such as where you're from or what you're passionate about. This personal touch helps establish a connection right from the start.

Next, quickly dive into the problem you're solving. While the solution may evolve over time, the problem remains constant. Highlighting the problem shows investors that you've identified a significant challenge worth tackling.

For example, consider Netflix's initial approach. If they had simply said they were building a DVD rental service, it wouldn't have grabbed investors' attentions. But by framing it as solving the problem of piracy through an on-demand platform, it sparked interest and provided a clear direction for the conversation.

Finally, wrap up your message with a call to action. Clearly state what you're seeking from the investor and why their time is valuable. This brings a sense of urgency and purpose to the conversation, making it more likely to lead to further discussions.

To summarize the above, we can say that one needs to include the following pointers in the cold message to the investor *(Aditya's three principles)*.

1. What is the problem you are solving?
2. Would it change the world if the problem gets solved?
3. Why are you the best person to solve this problem?

5. How to Assess the Amount of Funding You Need at a Particular Stage?

a. Make a Realistic Business Plan for twelve to eighteen months.
b. Extrapolate the profit/loss situation of the company till then.
c. Raise capital, which lets you hit your business plan targets while maintaining profitability.

6. What Do You Need to Provide to the Investor on Your Cold Message Being Accepted? Which Documents Are Required?

Before giving you an appointment, the investor would require certain information from you. They usually ask for a pitch deck, which is basically a presentation of your startup. This should be crisp and concise, not more than fifteen slides, and give out the entire gamut of your startup, The revenue model, strategies and plans, requirement of the investment and the utilization of the same should be covered in detail.

Secondly, financial projections need to be presented outlining the estimated business performance over a period of the next three to five years. This is usually presented in an Excel format. Remember, the investor is basically interested at the potential returns over the next few years, as their successful exit generally comes after eighteen to twenty-four months.

Therefore, the financial projections should depict the expected graph of the business showing the rate of growth, the time it will take to become profitable and whether this projected growth is in alignment with the fixed and variable costs of running your business.

7. How Many Rounds Does an Entrepreneur Have to Go Through to Convince an Investor?

Well, the first rule of startup investing is that there are no rules.

There is no set number. Just as there's no fixed number of dates to determine if a relationship will work out, the same goes for investor meetings in the startup world.

On average, it typically ranges from two to three rounds. Usually, the interest of the investor is invoked in the first meeting itself. Most of the convincing is done in the initial interactions. The later meetings only validate the initial interest and conviction. Investors mostly focus on the evident passion and confidence of the founders and the credibility of their pitch.

Now, closing a funding round typically takes about three months and follows this process:

1. Term-Sheet Issuance: The deal kicks off with the term sheet, outlining the investment's key terms like valuation, equity stake and special rights.
2. Due Diligence: The investor then conducts due diligence, evaluating the startup's financials, legal standing and operations to ensure everything aligns with expectations.
3. Signing of the Shareholder Agreement (SHA): Next, both parties sign the shareholder agreement, which solidifies ownership rights and responsibilities, along with exit strategies.
4. Capital Deployment: Finally, the agreed capital is transferred, typically in stages, to fuel the startup's growth.

Each investor may have their own approach and criteria for evaluating startups, and the number of meetings required to make a decision can vary greatly depending on the circumstances.

For early-stage deals, it may be usually a lesser number of meetings. For later-stages, it may be more.

8. Should You Raise Funding from One Investor or Multiple Investors?

The best approach would be to diversify your investor base. Spreading the investment across multiple backers can offer several benefits.

The advantages of diversifying the investor base include, firstly, mitigating the risk. Having multiple investors removes the dependency on a single entity for decisions. Secondly, it brings about a diverse set of perspectives and expertise. Different insights, networks and resources from various investors can add great value to your startup.

As Sunny Garg, co-founder of Crib, also said in the chapter on 'Bootstrapping Vs Fundraising', 'Don't put all your eggs in one basket.' One should be very cognizant of the risks associated with relying solely on one investor.

You might have seen on Shark Tank how founders always try to optimize, negotiating for better terms like offering more stake in the startup in exchange for an all-Shark Tank deal. The reason for this approach is simple: you want more people who can bring in more value at a lower cost. If you only raise funds from one investor, their expertise and resources may be limited. But if you raise funds from multiple investors, each specializing in different areas, they can collectively add more value to your startup.

The key difference between securing investment from an investor or from a bank is that banks focus on lending you money but an investor will focus on both lending you money and providing strategic guidance. While banks focus on a rotating average, investing in startups is about backing people's dreams.

It's not purely emotional, but there's definitely a human element to it.

9. How Do You Value Your Startup?

Jugaad By FAAD—Aditya Arora's Method of Valuation[2]

To illustrate how you can value your startup, a method of valuation as devised by my co-author, taken from his LinkedIn post, is described below.

Step 1: Estimate the minimum cash you need for the next twelve months. Add all your expenses and see what minimum you need to spend in these twelve months to achieve the desired growth. Any angel investment should have ten to twelve months of money left in the bank. Let us assume the number comes out to be Rs 1 crore.

Step 2: Estimate the amount of equity you need to dilute to raise this capital. Typically, in an early-stage round, founders can dilute anywhere between 5 per cent and 25 per cent easily. Estimate the future capital you will need and dilute accordingly. Let us say you want to give away 20 per cent.

Step 3: Voila, you just got to know your valuation. It will be total raised times 100 divided by dilution percentage or Rs 1 crore times (100/20) = Rs 5 crore (pre-money valuation). The post-money valuation would be Rs 5 crore + Rs 1 crore = Rs 6 crore.

10. Some Dos and Don'ts of Pitching

Dos of Pitching

1. Grab the attention of the investors at the first instance.
2. Focus on what investors want to hear.
3. Be to the point, clear and concise in your pitch.
4. Structure the pitch as a story.
5. End with a 'call to action' on what funding you need.

Don'ts of Pitching

1. Don't let it hurt your ego when confronted with questions by the investor.
2. Don't use too many technical terms or unfamiliar jargon.
3. Don't overcrowd your slides with lots of content.
4. Don't present information that can't be easily understood.
5. Don't ignore or gloss over the investors' questions.

From here on, as you venture into the world of entrepreneurship, remember that securing investment is not just about the money, but is also about aligning with the right partners who believe in your vision, share your passion and are willing to walk alongside you through the ups and downs. Choose wisely, pitch passionately and always stay true to your purpose—because your startup's future is in your hands, and with the right support, the possibilities are endless.

So, What Should You Do Next?

Pitch your startup to five people in less than 30 seconds and get a score out of 10. Keep doing this activity till you hit a combined score of at least 40.

15

Founders' Mindset to Grow Bigger

The Rise and Rise of Physics Wallah

Physics Wallah[1] *is an Indian multinational EdTech company aiming to provide affordable and quality education. Launched by Alakh Pandey in 2016 as a YouTube channel and later joined by Prateek Maheshwari, it was made into an app in 2020, offering JEE and NEET courses. In 2022, PW attained 'unicorn status' with a $1.1 billion valuation after a $100 million funding round. This marked the beginning of its offline expansion, with the launch of Vidyapeeth in Kota, Rajasthan—India's coaching hub. By November 2023, PW had established sixty-seven offline centres across thirty-four cities, blending online and offline learning experiences. Today, with a valuation of $2.8 billion as of September 2024, PW continues to transform India's affordable education landscape.*

This chapter is a culmination of all the ideas we have described so far in this book. In the first chapter, we looked at how ideation and finding the right problem to solve is the initial step of building a startup. In the other chapters, we looked at how to work on this idea, building an MVP (Minimum Viable Product) appropriately and then figuring out things such as pricing, distribution, acquisition, scaling and even fundraising.

But one crucial aspect of the startup world that is usually overlooked is how to build the right mindset, especially an 'incremental mindset'. You can build a million-dollar business with our other chapters, but how do you keep growing to become a unicorn valued in billions?

This chapter is not about how to build a million-dollar business but a million-dollar mindset, which will serve as a toolkit for the former.

In the last phase of the startup journey, where entrepreneurs are looking to scale up and achieve the so-far 'mission impossible', firstly the founders' mindset and secondly the organization's mindset plays a crucial role.

The Mindset Extraordinaire: The Founders' Mindset of Physics Wallah

The title of Jeff Keller's bestselling book, 'Attitude is Everything', is an apt phrase to introduce here. The book talks about how one should clean their 'attitude window', be receptive to new ideas and be malleable to the dynamics of the world. One should have a flexible mindset open to unlearning and learning requisite ideas. The Buddha's teachings and the Bhagwad Gita also give utmost importance to the right mindset and clarity of thought in the process of achieving the desired goal.

In our interaction with Prateek, co-founder of PW, it was evident that he had honed the 'right mindset' one needs to make a startup scale. Having worked on numerous startups earlier, he had seen and done it all. But what made him sail through the ups and downs of the startup journey was his ability to cut through the noise and focus on what really mattered. Yes, he had the mindset of a warrior—the one that helps the best become unique and stand out in the crowd.

Serendipity took Prateek to a chance meeting with Alakh, from where he embarked on his journey with PW.

Never in their wildest dreams had they thought that they would go on to build one of the most valuable EdTech companies in Bharat's startup ecosystem.

So, how did this merging of two 'not-so ordinary mindsets' converge into something of extraordinary value that would change the lives of students across Bharat?

To understand just that, let's take a walk on the paths taken by the two co-founders of PW.

The Physics Wallah Poem: Where Two Roads Converged

In his famous poem, 'The Road Not Taken', Robert Frost says:

Two roads diverged in a yellow wood,
And sorry I could not travel both
And be one traveller, long I stood

The Physics Wallah poem goes thus:
Two roads converged for a common good,
And thanks that we could travel the one made
And be co-travellers, as we always would
But the question is how?

First, let's look at Alakh's journey.

Alakh was in his third year at Harcourt Butler Technical University, Kanpur, when he realized his passion for teaching. Having taught students while in school, especially physics, he wanted to teach aspirants preparing for various competitive exams such as JEE and NEET. His passion for teaching was so strong that he applied to various coaching institutions, though he was always met with rejection. Nobody took him seriously!

The coaching institutions' responses usually were, '*Arre tu kya padhayega, teri toh khud padhne ki umar hai* [how will you teach, it is your age to learn].' Though dismayed by this response, he insisted and persisted that he was the right fit to teach kids and requested coaching institutions for a chance to take a demo class. And guess what? The demo classes had such an impact on students that they literally scrambled for them. Within a short period, these classes ran short of space for students. The classes kindled interest in the 'not-so-interested' students as well, who in coming times would find seats reserved in their dream colleges. Such was Alakh's charisma. He realized that he had the knack to make seemingly complicated concepts in physics fun. Students started loving his teaching style so much that they didn't want any other teacher for the physics subject. They just wanted to learn from the maestro himself.

As his student base increased, Alakh felt that he should reach millions of students across India, who were struggling to understand the nitty-gritties of subjects like physics and didn't have access to affordable coaching. He realized that YouTube could be a brilliant platform for this. With traditional teaching methods being the norm in India, Alakh thought of simple, innovative methods from daily life to clarify the concepts of physics. These were conveyed through his unique signature style *josh* [energy]. The resounding greeting of students at the start of the class left them all with no choice but to concentrate with full enthusiasm and *hosh* [concentration]. Alakh's content soon became very relatable to even a person who had no prior knowledge of the subject. Even a backbencher would say, '*Arre yaar, mazaa hi aa gaya*! [This is fun!]'. Soon, the community started growing, and PW became a name unto itself.

But how did this YouTube channel turn into a massive empire worth $2.8 billion, employing over 15,000 people?

That is where none other than Prateek enters. An IITian, Prateek had a lot of entrepreneurial experience. Having started multiple ventures across FoodTech and EdTech earlier, he had a strong understanding of the nuances of running a successful business venture. At the time of this beautiful convergence of what would become PW, he was working on a startup called PenPencil. They used to create technological and backend support for coaching institutions and educators. One day, Prateek emailed Alakh regarding how he could technically support his journey to cater to more students. At that time, Alakh was just a one-man army with massive distribution, and wanted to launch a mobile app for affordable courses. What started as Prateek being a tech partner for Alakh's mission to provide affordable education would soon redefine education forever. And it wouldn't be wrong to say that this collaboration was not merely a coincidence—it was destined that physics got its much-needed tools, the PenPencil.

While Prateek's company, PenPencil, had managed 5000 concurrent users in a live class before, he told Alakh that he could build a tech product that would handle the same number of users for the latter's classes as well. This was the time of the Covid-19 pandemic, when everything went online. Not in their wildest dreams did the duo ever think that they would actually need to handle a class of more than 5000 people, but as luck always favours the brave, 50,000 students joined the live class. This incident resulted in the app crashing. This was eerily similar to the students 'crashing' Alakh's offline courses. Alakh was upset about this and wanted to refund the money to the students, but Prateek convinced him that he would rebuild the entire technical engine, do the growth testing and rebuild the DevOps as a whole. Soon, he was able to get everything to work correctly and win Alakh's trust and confidence.

The Internet was designed to make things more accessible, especially education, but the high costs of courses in the EdTech space proved to be to the contrary. This brought into focus the aspect of 'affordability', if it was to appeal to students of all strata of society. This gap was the core issue addressed by PW, which helped the offering permeate to all corners of the country, making it one of the leading players in its space.

Till 2020, Alakh had made a massive online community with his YouTube channel. During Covid-19, the availability of teachers for online classes increased as people were confined within the walls of their homes and had all the time for any online tasks. Coincidentally, PW was one of the largest online communities and platforms and hence, attracted a lot of teachers. From 2020 to 2021, over 1.5 lakh paid users were acquired by PW, and over $3 million in revenue was generated. The staggering demand for medical and engineering courses in India spurred PW to address this demand with affordable and quality online content and classes.

Being endowed with exceptional mindsets, PW had the ability to visualize the market beyond the pandemic. The duo knew that the personal touch and interaction of physical classes would also have to be catered to later, and this foresight gave birth to the hybrid model of Pathshala. The live scheduled classes in these Pathshalas have subject-level associate faculties with a limited batch size to focus on every student. This model was inspired by China's 'Two-Teacher System'.

But this hybrid model posed a whole new set of challenges. The launch of PW Pathshalas (physical learning centres) required an entirely different strategy. Renting real estate, hiring in-person educators and managing day-to-day operations led to higher operating expenses and logistical challenges.

Keeping the 'Student's Interest' at the Core

Prateek says, 'We were never focused on building a large business. It happened because we stayed true to our core values and mission of solving the affordability problem in education.'

This guiding philosophy shaped every decision made at PW. At the time they were raising $100 million, **PW's daily engagement metrics were a whopping 2 lakh**

students clocking in 100 minutes of daily engagement. Such numbers were impressive and unprecedented in the global education space.

Also, with the resounding success of its physics batches for JEE and NEET, they decided to expand into other verticals and exams, including UPSC, GATE, MBA, etc.

For PW, the 'product' was not a simple course or video series. It was an entire learning ecosystem built around a 'batch'. This system included carefully planned curriculum and pacing guides, daily practice problems (DPPs) and fortnightly tests.

As you read through this chapter and the pages of this book, remember that the journey of Physics Wallah has never been a cakewalk. They faced many, many challenges — yes, *many* of them!

Not every day will be a win. Where there are wins, there are also losses, too!

Back in the day, PW even tried venturing into the market of doubt-solving. In India, students often have a large number of doubts, but don't have the right mentors to solve these doubts for them. But here comes the problem: the solutions to most of the students' questions are already on the web.

While the team at PW initially believed that the idea would work, they soon realized that students in India would never pay for doubt-solving services. In India, students prefer to get the same value at zero cost if something is free. Students are willing to pay for learning outcomes but not for doubt resolution. This reality hit them hard, eventually leading to a shutdown of the idea.

As they say in startups, it's not just about which idea wins or which has potential—it's also about knowing when to pursue or abandon an idea at the right time. You need the right mindset and a clear frame of mind to make tough decisions and remain at peace with them. Not everyone possesses this ability, but it is essential for a startup's growth and survival.

In our societies, we often ridicule, shame and taunt those who quit. But in business, startups and even life, quitting isn't always a sign of failure—sometimes, it's a necessity. Quitting at the right time can open doors you never imagined existed. This doesn't mean you shut down entirely and abandon everything you were doing. It means you recognize when to kill an idea and pivot to one that's better suited to market needs and aligned with the core philosophy you're striving to build for.

As a founder, you shouldn't be ego-driven. You should not make things up in your head or not listen to reality just because of your ego. Sacrificing is very important. As a founder, you have to listen to the data and what the market wants.

As a founder, tyaag karna kai baar anivarya ho jata hai [making sacrifices becomes inevitable].

You also need to develop the 'not everything will work' mindset. It is this very mindset that has propelled PW to a team of over 15,000 employees and a community of 5.5 million students.

However, the founders' mindset alone is not enough. Building the right team with the right mindset, vision alignment and mission alignment is also crucial.

So, how does PW motivate its teachers and align them with the core value of student love?

PW believes in serving the bottom of the pyramid by providing affordable, high-quality education. When students from this group succeed, it motivates the entire organization, including teachers and educators, to give their best. This sense of ownership and accomplishment stems from knowing that they are contributing to society.

What the founders have learned from building PW is that culture can't be faked. They never viewed students as customers; students are the heart of the organization. These values are continuously reinforced in leadership and the culture naturally spreads from the top down.

Once the core values and philosophy were reinforced in every meeting, the thinking permeated the culture and gradually took shape. On day zero, the founders didn't know what culture was or whether they were building one, but as the organization grew, everyone began to listen to their hearts—the hearts of the students. PW evolved into a student-outcome-focused company with a strong emphasis on innovation.

Today, PW is a much larger organization; as it grows, staying agile becomes more challenging.

But how do you encourage agility and innovation as you scale?

This is a question every founder faces. The propagation of culture becomes more challenging with growth, but with the right tools, motivating teams in the right way and aligning the vision, things fall into place. Despite being a bit slower than in the early days, PW is now a responsible, data-driven, informed and confident company.

Prateek, during our conversation, said, 'The difference is like that between a teenager and someone in their twenties—from being quick and spontaneous in the initial days to becoming more responsible and thoughtful today, a slight but significant shift.'

Scaling a startup from a small team to a massive organization with over 15,000 employees is a remarkable transformation, and every founder must learn how to adapt to such change.

Time Is the Biggest Teacher, and Being Hands-On Is the Key

Even Rome wasn't built in a day. What worked for PW is being hands-on—you can't distance yourself from your customers too early on.

It's always very fruitful to stay hands-on.

Of course, over time, an entrepreneur realizes which things are most important and should be given utmost priority and which aren't as crucial and can be handled by other leaders in the organization. But that's something only time teaches you; no course, book or person can teach you that—only time can.

One thing Prateek firmly believes in and has witnessed himself, along with Alakh, is that the scale of a company truly transforms you as a person. During our conversation with Prateek, he said, 'You need to have trust in delegation; you must trust your teams. You must develop the ability to delegate without micromanaging because if you micromanage too much, the company will not be able to grow. But as you grow your company and evolve yourself, don't overthink or stress too much. Trust your gut and keep moving forward. There's one more thing I would like to add: pivots are often based on gut feeling, not always on data. From my experience with my earlier startup in the EdTech market (PenPencil) and with PW, I was able to dissect the problem, build the backend with Alakh and scale PW to where it is today.'

As they say, '*Dil ka raasta pet se hota hai* [The way to the heart is through the stomach].' In the same way, 'A founder's mindset *ka raasta uski gut se hota hai*! [The way to the founder's mindset is through their gut!]'

In the zero-to-one journey of a startup, you have to think outside the box. You need to be an unconventional leader and solve problems.

During our interaction, Prateek said, 'I knew that I was good at zero to one, but I knew I needed to find someone to help us scale from one to ten. That is how we built our teams, and that is how we set the right culture—motivating people, giving them a goal, making them feel at home and bringing them closer to the mission of solving for education and affordability.'

Today, PW is no ordinary institution. It is an organization with a purpose and a value system—offering the most affordable exam prep courses and materials for various exams like GATE, UPSC, NEET, IITJEE and more. Additionally, it has evolved into a full-fledged company with diverse offerings, including the Institute of Innovation (IOI), the School of Startups (SOS), skilling programs, higher education, study-abroad services, etc.

Lessons from the Founders' Mindset

1. Always develop a customer-centric approach.
2. Always ensure flexibility and adaptation.
3. Focus on your core and build from there.
4. Keep innovating through feedback.
5. Small wins matter; don't let others tell you otherwise.

The story of Alakh and Prateek is a masterclass in grit, flexibility and a relentless focus on value creation. The founders' mindset—the warrior-like ability to persist despite setbacks—drove them to reimagine education for millions of students across Bharat.

Key Takeaways

- Start with a Clear Mission.
- Adopt a Growth-Oriented Mindset.
- Build a Culture of Ownership.
- Focus on the Community, Not Just Customers.
- Move from a Product to a System.
- Don't Chase Money, Chase Impact.
- Dream Big, Act Bold.
- Resilience Matters.
- Communication Is a Superpower.

So, What Should You Do Next?

Write down your five weak points as a founder and write solutions for ones you can address. Consult someone trustworthy to work on those for whom you could not write solutions.

Also, you can read the following books to learn more about culture, organizational building and mindset:

1. *The Hard Thing About Hard Things* by Ben Horowitz
2. *High Output Management* by Andrew S. Grove
3. *Start with Why* by Simon Sinek
4. *Atomic Habits* by James Clear

Also, like in the previous chapters, given below is the framework called RISING, which will guide you through Physics Wallah's journey in a nutshell:

Roadblock	**Ideal Customer**	**Solution**	**Innovation**	**Nakad (Money)**	**Growth**
High-cost, inaccessible education for tier-2/3 students	Students from tier-2/3 cities and rural India	Affordable EdTech platform offering live classes, video lectures and doubt-solving	Ultra-low course fees to make education affordable Batch-based learning system for structured progress Personalized learning paths and doubt-solving support	Revenue from affordable course fees for JEE/NEET/UPSC/GATE/MBA and other competitive exams Adoption of a freemium model for select content (YouTube channel) to increase funnel size	- Diversification into exams like UPSC, GATE and MBA to increase TAM (Total Addressable Market) Launched offline PW Pathshalas for hybrid learning Leveraged the ' students-first' approach to increase loyalty and referrals

Roadblock	Ideal Customer	Solution	Innovation	Nakad (Money)	Growth
Traditional coaching was location-dependent	Students seeking flexibility to study anytime, anywhere	Mobile-first learning platform accessible on phones, tablets and desktops	On-demand video content for 24/7 learning Live classes accessible via low-bandwidth connections Custom tech stack for seamless content delivery even in low-Internet areas	Paid subscriptions to pre-recorded video lectures and crash courses Ad revenue from free YouTube content (brand collaborations, etc.)	YouTube-first approach to establish brand trust and acquire early users Word-of-mouth referrals from satisfied students and parents Cross-sell and upsell advanced courses (like crash courses for exams)

Closing Note

Startups of Bharat

Congratulations! You have finally passed all fifteen levels of the simulation.

We hope that you enjoyed reading this book as much as we enjoyed writing it. All the fifteen chapters were so interesting to build up, and it was painful to hear the hardships of these entrepreneurs while they were narrating their stories to us. Again, we thank them for being candid, upfront and honest in sharing their life's highs and lows with the same smile on their face. The stories shared within these pages are not just narratives—they are testaments to the human spirit, to the boundless possibilities that await when passion meets perseverance and to the transformative power of ideas brought to life.

Many other inspiring entrepreneurs have built massive companies, but unfortunately, we cannot cover them in this book. India is just full of so many young and enterprising minds. But hey, maybe a second version of this book?

Why not? We love writing stories. But we would need your support too. If you liked this book, share it on your social media. We will be happy to share the post. Please tag @adi_arora and @thesuryapasricha on Instagram.

If you want a promising entrepreneur to read this book, gift it to them. If not, DM us; maybe we can figure out a way. Seriously, we want this book to reach the masses. India has about 1,17,254 startups as per DPIIT, as on 31 December 2023.[1] Indeed, this data may be outdated, but India needs more. Much, much, much more. This will come from people below thirty-five, representing 66 per cent of India's population.[2] And this book is a step in that direction.

And it would not have been possible without Manish Khurana and Saba Nehal from Penguin—our dream publishers and a dream team to work with. Also, a big thanks to our colleagues, Dr Dinesh Singh, Karan Verma, Aditya's partners at FAAD Capital along with the entire FAAD team, and Harshika Paliwal, who helped us crack the very first interview of this book with Neetu from Animall. We also thank Dr Sandeep Goyal—renowned Indian adman, MD of Rediffusion, and himself a leading author—who played a pivotal role in inspiring Surya to embark on his writing journey, drawing from his remarkable work and books. Our gratitude extends to Reena Singh and Mansi Chauhan from Magnon TBWA, Surya's first mentors, for providing invaluable guidance during his early steps in the industry and to the entire team at BaatCheet Media for their for their continued support and helping out with the illustrations and tables. A big thanks to our parents for serving lip-smacking food whenever we used to be in each other's houses for brainstorming.

While we wanted to capture the stories of many other remarkable young entrepreneurs, we could only focus on a handful of the book. But perhaps there's a sequel waiting to happen?

We would like to give a shoutout to some of these fantastic entrepreneurs: Sparsh from Stylework, Hardik Bhatia from SustVest, Sarthak Jain from Findr, Darshan Shah from NewsReach, Harshita Kejriwal from Basil, Devansh Agarwal from Peppy and many more. Keep inspiring, guys; we look forward to publishing you soon.

Also, one final thought to readers before we end this:

Seize every opportunity to learn and grow. Take advantage of live projects, internships and networking events. After all, I (Aditya Arora) was an intern at the company which I am now heading as the CEO. Startups teach us something, no matter the age!

As we turn to the final sentence of this page, let us carry forward the lessons learned, the inspiration garnered and the connections forged. To Startup India, Standup India, India for the World and Startups of Bharat!

Notes

Foreword

1 Meha Agarwal, '2019 In Review: What Indian Unicorns Were Up To This Year', Inc42, 17 December 2019, https://inc42.com/features/2019-in-review-the-year-gone-by-for-indian-startup-unicorns/.

2 Rajiv Bhuva, 'India's unicorns have created a whopping 2.84 million jobs', YourStory, https://yourstory.com/2022/05/startup-100-unicorns-india-job-creation.

3 '10 million jobs must be created by India every year', Finance Story, 1 November 2024, https://thefinancestory.com/india-must-create-10-mn-jobs-by-2030-says-goldman-sachs.

4 'India is youngest start-up nation with 72% founders below 35 years: Nirmala Sitharaman', *Business Standard*, 23 July 2016, https://www.business-standard.com/article/economy-policy/india-is-youngest-start-up-nation-with-72-founders-below-35-years-nirmala-sitharaman-116072300644_1.html.

5 Trisha Tewari, '32.5% Indian students want to become startup owners: 5 reasons fuelling their entrepreneurial

dreams', *Times of* India, 22 October 2024, https://timesofindia.indiatimes.com/education/news/32-5-indian-students-want-to-establish-become-startup-owners-5-reasons-that-fuel-their-entrepreneurial-aspirations/articleshow/114465999.cms.

1. It All Begins with a Problem: The Story of Animall from 0 to Rs 4000 Crore in Transaction Value

1 https://animall.in/.
2 'India - Rural Population (% of Total Population)', Trading Economics, November 2024, https://tradingeconomics.com/india/rural-population-percent-of-total-population-wb-data.html.
3 Sandhya Keelery, 'Cattle population in India 2016–2024,' Statista (28 June 2024), available at https://www.statista.com/statistics/1181408/india-cattle-population/.
4 Sandeep Goyal, 'Indian ad man and managing director of Rediffusion', Rediff.com (14 August, 2023), https://www.rediff.com/getahead/report/what-you-must-know-about-animall-app/20230814.htm.

2. The Million-Dollar Idea: How Did bluelearn Scale to 1,50,000 Members?

1 https://www.bluelearn.in/.
2 https://www.youtube.com/watch?v=tBJWOzZNQ5A; https://youtu.be/tBJWOzZNQ5A?si=wLQMiI97-fBzwvHU; https://youtu.be/gehLhcBKh6o?si=Q2L-SLsFcGUGIarp.
3 Steve Jobs, 'Stay hungry, stay foolish', Stanford University Commencement Address, YouTube, https://www.youtube.com/watch?v=UF8uR6Z6KLc.

4 '62 Albert Schweitzer Quotes (On Life, Gratitude, Service)', Wisdom Quotes, https://wisdomquotes.com/albert-schweitzer-quotes/.

3. Prototype from Scratch: Inside View of Pepper Content to Scale to 1,20,000-Plus Creators

1 https://www.peppercontent.io/.
2 William L. Hosch, 'YouTube', Britannica, https://www.britannica.com/topic/YouTube.
3 'Google buys YouTube for $1.65 billion', NBC News, 6 October 2006, https://www.nbcnews.com/id/wbna15196982.
4 'Pepper Content: How 23-year-old Anirudh Singla built one of India's largest content platforms', Global Indian, 5 March 2024, https://www.globalindian.com/youth/story/entrepreneur/anirudh-singla-the-teen-who-built-one-of-indias-largest-content-platforms/.
5 'About us', Pepper Content, https://www.peppercontent.io/about-us/.

4. Do I Need Technology?: The VC-Funded Startup Expand My Business

1 See more about Expand My Business at 'Expand My Business', YourStory, https://yourstory.com/companies/expand-my-business and EMB Global, https://www.emb.global/.
2 AIESEC (Association Internationale Des Étudiants en Sciences Économiques et Commerciales or the International Association of Students in Economics and Business) is a global youth platform for leadership

and development through practical experiences such as internships and volunteering opportunities.

3 Toastmasters International is a nonprofit educational organization that builds confidence and teaches public-speaking skills through a worldwide network of clubs that meet online and in person. In a supportive community or corporate environment, members prepare and deliver speeches, respond to impromptu questions, and give and receive constructive feedback. It is through this regular practice that members are empowered to meet personal and professional communication goals. Founded in 1924, the organization is headquartered in Englewood, Colorado with approximately 2,70,000 members in more than 14,000 clubs in 150 countries.

4 Young-Chan Kim, 'Alibaba: Jack Ma's Unique Growth Strategy and the Future of Its Global Development in the Chinese Digital Business Industry: Exploring the Transformation from Manufacturing to a Digital Service Hub' (2018), https://www.researchgate.net/publication/326515609_Alibaba_Jack_Ma's_Unique_Growth_Strategy_and_the_Future_of_Its_Global_Development_in_the_Chinese_Digital_Business_Industry_Exploring_the_Transformation_from_Manufacturing_to_a_Digital_Service_Hub.

5 EMB Global, https://www.emb.global/.

5. Solo Date or Mentorship?: The Tale of a 100-Million-Dollar Startup Founder

1 https://tanx.fi/.

2 'mentor', Oxford English Dictionary, https://www.oed.com/dictionary/mentor_n?tab=meaning_and_use.

6. Right Team, Culture and ESOPs: Odyssey of GrowthSchool

1 https://growthschool.io/.

2 Kartikay Kashyap, 'ESOP Buybacks: 3,000+ Startup Employees Made Over INR 1,450 Cr In 2024', Inc42, 15 December 2024, https://inc42.com/features/esop-buybacks-3000-startup-employees-made-over-inr-1450-cr-in-2024/.

3 'Flipkart employees to receive cash payout from $700m Esop buyback', *Business Standard*, 7 July 2023, https://www.business-standard.com/companies/news/flipkart-employees-to-receive-cash-payout-from-700m-esop-buyback-123070700349_1.html.

4 Nikhil Kamath podcast on YouTube, 'WTF Ep# 16 | What character "flaws" make the best entrepreneurs? Nikhil ft. Ritesh, Ghazal and Manish', YouTube, 6 March 2024, https://youtu.be/FPV5fAkqyBs?si=axmVLY0nqejIpw91.

5 Reed Hastings and Erin Meyer, No Rules Rules: Netflix and the Culture of Reinvention, https://www.norulesrules.com/.

7. Register in India Versus Outside: Crest's Homecoming to India

1 https://www.getcrest.ai/.

2 ZenBusiness, 'Fastest Unicorn Companies', https://www.zenbusiness.com/fastest-unicorns/.

3 'Unicorns Of Tomorrow Decoding India's Soonicorn Landscape Report, 2024', Inc42, https://inc42.com/reports/unicorns-of-tomorrow-decoding-indias-soonicorn-landscape-report-2024/?login=1; GoI Startup

India website, https://www.startupindia.gov.in/content/sih/en/startup-scheme.html; 'The Indian Unicorn Landscape', Invest India, https://www.investindia.gov.in/indian-unicorn-landscape.

4 'The Indian Unicorn Landscape', Invest India, https://www.investindia.gov.in/indian-unicorn-landscape.

5 Inc42, '5 Indian Startup Hubs that Received the Most Funding in Q1 2024', https://inc42.com/web-stories/5-most-funded-indian-startup-hubs-of-q1-2024/.

6 Aditya Rangroo, '90 founders among 500 US unicorns were India born: Study', ETtech of *Economic Times* (15 January 2022), https://economictimes.indiatimes.com/tech/startups/90-founders-among-500-us-unicorns-were-india-born-study/articleshow/88919258.cms?from=mdr.

7 Indiaspora Impact Report, 'Small Community, Big Contributions, Boundless Horizons: The Indian Diaspora in the United States', https://www.indiaspora.org/full-impact-report/.

8 More about the book: https://www.attitudeiseverything.com/.

8. Know Your Customer (KYC): The Thrilling Narrative of Chai Sutta Bar

1 https://www.chaisuttabarindia.com/.

2 UN's 2024 Revision of World Population Prospects Report: https://population.un.org/wpp/.

3 https://www.youtube.com/@thebarbershopwithshantanu6670.

4 https://www.bombayshavingcompany.com/.

5 https://www.chaisuttabarindia.com/.

9. Acquiring Your First 100 Customers : The Journey of the Unicorn, BharatPe

1 https://bharatpe.com/.
2 Adam Hayes, 'Tulipmania: About the Dutch Tulip Bulb Market Bubble', Investopedia, (25 June 2024), https://www.investopedia.com/terms/d/dutch_tulip_bulb_market_bubble.asp.

10. Pricing, the Holy Grail of Business: How Does Boult Sell Products Every Three Seconds?

1 https://www.boultaudio.com/.
2 Xbox Pricing - https://navi.com/blog/price-skimming/.
3 Netflix pricing - https://www.businessworld.in/article/netflix-india-plans-gets-price-cut-check-out-new-plans-414730.

11. Skyrocketing Your Distribution: The Sneakerhead Who Sells to Ranbir Kapoor and Ranveer Singh

1 https://marketplace.mainstreet.co.in/.
2 @VedantLamba on YouTube: https://www.youtube.com/@vedantlamba.
3 Mainstreet Marketplace's YouTube Channel (called Mainstreet TV): https://www.youtube.com/@MainStreettv.

12. Retaining Your Customer: Take from an AI Mobile Keyboard Company with 100 Million Users

1 Bobble AI's Website: https://bobble.ai/en/home.

2 Bobble AI's valuation: https://tracxn.com/d/companies/bobble-ai/__I51xSifn5jrTbDN2wrpE8Kdm6CjxaeyrF_sNBlIhxC8#:~:text=The%20latest%20valuation%20of%20Bobble,as%20on%20Apr%2021%2C%202023. Tracxn, 'Bobble AI funding & investors', 16 November 2024, https://tracxn.com/d/companies/bobble-ai/__I51xSifn5jrTbDN2wrpE8Kdm6CjxaeyrF_sNBlIhxC8/funding-and-investors.

3 Scott Scrivens, 'Google Indic Keyboard reaches 100 million downloads, despite being eclipsed by Gboard', Android Police, (4 October 2017), https://www.androidpolice.com/2017/10/04/google-indic-keyboard-reaches-100-million-downloads-despite-eclipsed-gboard/.

4 Blogs:
1. https://solsten.io/blog/d1-d7-d30-retention-in-gaming.
2. https://www.mistplay.com/resources/mobile-app-user-retention-metrics.
3. https://growthbug.com/what-retention-metric-you-should-be-measuring-1e5330df0088.

13. Bootstrapping Versus Fundraising: Multimillion-Dollar Exit and Raising Funds from Founders of CRED, Paytm and Mamaearth

1 'One of its kind housing brand Your Shell has been acquired by Stanza Living', *Forbes* India, (17 September 2020), https://www.forbesindia.com/article/brand-

connect/one-of-its-kind-housing-brand-your-shell-has-been-acquired-by-stanza-living/62685/1.

14. A Rookie's Guide to Raising Funds: A Special Investor's Take

1 'The State Of Indian Startup Ecosystem Report 2024', Inc42, https://inc42.com/reports/the-state-of-indian-startup-ecosystem-report-2024/?itm_medium=website&itm_source=company-profile&itm_campaign=stories-tab&itm_content=article&itm_term=1.
2 Aditya Arora, 'The "Jugaad" Method of Valuation', LinkedIn, https://www.linkedin.com/posts/thefaadguy_founders-startup-bank-activity-7068829444089483264-Dl-e?utm_source=share&utm_medium=member_desktop.

15. Founders' Mindset to Grow Bigger: The Rise and Rise of Physics Wallah

1 https://www.pw.live/.

Closing Note: Startups of Bharat

1 Number of Startups - https://pib.gov.in/PressReleaseIframePage.aspx?PRID=2002100.
2 Population - https://www.ncesc.com/geographic-pedia/what-percentage-of-indias-population-is-under-25-years-old/.

Scan QR code to access the
Penguin Random House India website